LangGraph.js

A Hands-On Guide to Building Agent Workflows and Multi-Agent Systems in Web and Node.js Environments

©

Written By

Morgan Devline

Copyright

LangGraph.js: A Hands-On Guide to Building Agent Workflows and Multi-Agent Systems in Web and Node.js Environments
© 2024 Morgan Devline
All rights reserved.

No part of this publication may be reproduced, distributed, or transmitted in any form or by any means, including photocopying, recording, or other electronic or mechanical methods, without the prior written permission of the publisher, except in the case of brief quotations embodied in critical reviews and certain other noncommercial uses permitted by copyright law.

Disclaimer:
The information in this book is provided "as is" without any warranties or guarantees, express or implied. While every effort has been made to ensure the accuracy of the information provided, neither the author nor the publisher will be held responsible for any errors or omissions or for any damages arising from the use of the information in this book.

Acknowledgments:
I would like to thank all those who contributed to the creation of this book.

Table of Content

Introduction 6
    1. What is LangGraph.js? 6
    2. Who is This Book For? 9
    3. How to Use This Book 11
    4. Quick Start: Your First LangGraph.js Workflow in 15 Minutes ... 14

Chapter 1: Getting Started with LangGraph.js 23
    1.1 Understanding Agent Workflows and Multi-Agent Systems 23
    1.2 Setting Up LangGraph.js 26
    2.3 Your First Agent Workflow 30

Chapter 2: Core Concepts of LangGraph.js 41
    2.1 Agents and Workflows 41
    2.2 Nodes and Graphs 44
    2.3 Asynchronous Processing 47
    2.4 Mini-Project: Creating a Workflow to Fetch and Process API Data 58

Chapter 3: Building Intelligent Agents 71
    3.1 Agent Architectures 71
    3.2 Agent Communication and Messaging 75
    3.3 Error Handling in Workflows 81

Chapter 4: Scaling Multi-Agent Systems 89
    4.1 Scaling Workflows for Performance 89
    4.2 Workflow Orchestration 93
    4.3 Debugging and Testing Multi-Agent Systems 96

Chapter 5: Integrating LangGraph.js with Web Applications 100
    5.1 Frontend Integrations 100
    5.2 Backend Integrations 106
    5.3 Real-Time Applications 111

Chapter 6: Advanced Features of LangGraph.js 114
- 6.1 Custom Nodes and Agents 114
- 6.2 Performance Optimization 117
- 6.3 Workflow Automation 121

Chapter 7: Security in Multi-Agent Systems 126
- 7.1 Securing Agent Communication 126
- 7.2 Authentication and Authorization 130
- 7.3 Handling Malicious Agents 134

Chapter 8: Deploying LangGraph.js Applications 138
- 8.1 Deployment Strategies 138
- 8.2 Continuous Integration and Deployment 142
- 8.3 Monitoring and Observability 146

Chapter 9: Industry Applications of LangGraph.js 151
- 9.1 E-Commerce 151
- 9.2 Financial Services 154
- 9.3 AI-Powered Applications 158

Chapter 10: Exploring Creative Applications of LangGraph.js 163
- 10.1 Art and Music 163
- 10.2 Gaming and Simulations 167
- 10.3 Experimental Multi-Agent Workflows 171

Chapter 11: Hands-On Projects 175
- 11.1 Real-Time Chat Application 175
- 11.2 IoT Monitoring Workflow 181
- 11.3 E-Commerce Recommendation System 184

Chapter 12: Extending LangGraph.js 187
- 12.1 Contributing to LangGraph.js 187
- 12.2 Using LangGraph.js with Other Libraries 190
- 12.3 Building the LangGraph.js Ecosystem 194

Chapter 13: Interactive Learning with LangGraph.js 197

    13.1 Using CodeSandbox or StackBlitz..................................197

    13.2 Interactive Exercises 201

    13.3 Gamified Challenges for Workflow Design 205

Chapter 14: The Future of Agent Workflows..207

    14.1 Emerging Trends 207

    14.2 LangGraph.js Roadmap 211

Appendices..215

    Appendix A: LangGraph.js API Reference 215

    Appendix C: Resources and Further Reading 219

    Appendix D: Cheat Sheets..220

    Appendix E: Glossary of Terms...222

Conclusion...223

Introduction

Whether you're a seasoned developer looking to enhance your skill set or a newcomer eager to dive into the world of agent workflows, this book is designed to equip you with the knowledge and practical experience needed to master LangGraph.js. In this introduction, we'll explore what LangGraph.js is, who this book is intended for, how to effectively use this guide, and provide a quick start to get you up and running with your first LangGraph.js workflow in just 15 minutes.

1. What is LangGraph.js?

Understanding LangGraph.js is the foundation of this book. This section delves into the evolution of agent workflows, the importance of LangGraph.js in modern development, and an overview of its ecosystem.

The Evolution of Agent Workflows

Agent workflows have become integral in today's software development landscape, especially with the rise of distributed systems and artificial intelligence. Initially, workflows were linear and straightforward, suitable for simple tasks. However, as applications grew in complexity, the need for more dynamic and responsive systems emerged.

Early Workflow Systems:

- **Linear Workflows:** Simple, step-by-step processes where each step follows the previous one in a fixed order.
- **Manual Coordination:** Early systems required significant human intervention to manage workflows, limiting scalability and efficiency.

The Rise of Multi-Agent Systems:

- **Parallel Processing:** Introduction of workflows where multiple agents operate simultaneously, increasing efficiency.

- **Autonomous Agents:** Development of agents that can make independent decisions based on predefined rules and real-time data.
- **Inter-Agent Communication:** Enhanced systems where agents communicate and collaborate to achieve complex objectives.

Modern Agent Workflows:

- **Distributed Systems:** Workflows spread across multiple servers or environments, enhancing reliability and scalability.
- **AI Integration:** Incorporating artificial intelligence to enable agents to learn and adapt, improving decision-making and task execution.

Why LangGraph.js is Essential for Modern Development

LangGraph.js stands out as a powerful tool for building agent workflows and multi-agent systems, offering several advantages that make it essential for contemporary development practices.

Key Benefits:

- **Flexibility:** LangGraph.js allows developers to design complex workflows with ease, accommodating a wide range of applications from simple task automation to sophisticated AI-driven systems.
- **Scalability:** The framework supports scaling workflows horizontally, ensuring that applications can handle increasing loads without compromising performance.
- **Integration:** Seamlessly integrates with popular web frameworks and Node.js, enabling developers to incorporate agent workflows into existing projects effortlessly.
- **Community and Support:** Backed by an active community, LangGraph.js provides extensive resources, plugins, and support, facilitating continuous learning and problem-solving.

Real-World Applications:

- **E-Commerce:** Automating inventory management and order processing.
- **Financial Services:** Implementing fraud detection and real-time transaction monitoring.
- **AI-Powered Applications:** Developing chatbots and intelligent recommendation systems.

Practical Example: Imagine an e-commerce platform where LangGraph.js automates inventory updates, processes customer orders, and handles fraud detection simultaneously. This multi-agent system ensures seamless operations, reduces manual intervention, and enhances customer satisfaction.

Overview of the LangGraph.js Ecosystem

LangGraph.js is not just a standalone library; it's part of a broader ecosystem that enhances its functionality and usability. Understanding this ecosystem is crucial for leveraging LangGraph.js effectively.

Core Components:

- **LangGraph.js Library:** The main framework for building and managing agent workflows.
- **Plugins and Extensions:** Additional modules that extend the core functionality, such as database connectors, messaging systems, and AI integrations.
- **Development Tools:** Tools like code editors, debuggers, and testing frameworks that streamline the development process.

Integration with Other Technologies:

- **Node.js:** Provides a robust runtime environment, enabling server-side execution of LangGraph.js workflows.
- **Web Frameworks:** Integration with frameworks like Express.js and React.js allows for building full-stack applications that incorporate agent workflows seamlessly.

- **Databases:** Support for various databases (e.g., MongoDB, PostgreSQL) facilitates data management within workflows.
- **AI and Machine Learning Libraries:** Integration with libraries like TensorFlow.js and Brain.js enhances the intelligence and adaptability of agents.

Community and Resources:

- **Official Documentation:** Comprehensive guides and references to help developers get started and solve specific problems.
- **Forums and Discussion Groups:** Platforms like GitHub, Stack Overflow, and dedicated LangGraph.js forums where developers can seek help and share knowledge.
- **Tutorials and Courses:** A wealth of tutorials, online courses, and workshops that provide step-by-step instructions and practical insights.

2. Who is This Book For?

This book is tailored to a diverse audience, ensuring that both beginners and experienced developers can benefit from its content. Understanding who the book is for will help you navigate the material more effectively.

Web Developers

Web developers seeking to enhance their applications with intelligent agent workflows will find this book invaluable. Whether you're working on frontend, backend, or full-stack projects, LangGraph.js offers tools to build dynamic and responsive systems.

Key Topics for Web Developers:

- Integrating LangGraph.js with frontend frameworks like React.js.
- Building interactive dashboards for monitoring agent activities.
- Creating real-time applications such as chatbots and live notifications.

Practical Example: A web developer can use LangGraph.js to create a live notification system that updates users in real-time based on their interactions and data changes.

2Node.js Engineers

Node.js engineers looking to incorporate advanced workflow automation and multi-agent systems into their backend services will find comprehensive guidance in this book. LangGraph.js leverages the strengths of Node.js to deliver scalable and efficient workflows.

Key Topics for Node.js Engineers:

- Setting up LangGraph.js within a Node.js environment.
- Building and deploying backend services that utilize agent workflows.
- Ensuring scalability and performance of multi-agent systems in production.

Practical Example: A Node.js engineer can develop a fraud detection system that processes transactions in real-time, identifying and flagging suspicious activities using LangGraph.js.

AI and Multi-Agent System Enthusiasts

For those passionate about artificial intelligence and multi-agent systems, this book provides the tools and knowledge to build intelligent and autonomous agents. LangGraph.js serves as a bridge between AI concepts and practical application development.

Key Topics for AI Enthusiasts:

- Designing intelligent agents that learn and adapt.
- Implementing communication protocols between agents.
- Integrating AI and machine learning libraries to enhance agent capabilities.

Practical Example: An AI enthusiast can create a multi-agent system where each agent specializes in different aspects of natural language processing, working together to provide comprehensive language understanding and responses.

3. How to Use This Book

To maximize your learning experience, it's essential to understand how to navigate and utilize the resources provided in this book effectively. This section outlines the hands-on approach, required tools, prerequisites, and steps to set up your development environment.

Hands-On Approach

This book adopts a hands-on approach, emphasizing practical application alongside theoretical knowledge. Each chapter includes:

- **Conceptual Explanations:** Clear and concise explanations of key concepts.
- **Code Examples:** Real-world code snippets that demonstrate how to implement the discussed topics.
- **Projects and Exercises:** Engaging projects and exercises that allow you to apply what you've learned.

Benefit: This approach ensures that you not only understand the concepts but also gain the practical skills needed to implement them in real-world scenarios.

Tools and Prerequisites

Before diving into LangGraph.js, ensure you have the following tools and prerequisites:

Essential Tools:

- **Node.js:** Ensure you have Node.js installed (version X.X.X or later). Download Node.js
- **npm or Yarn:** Package managers for managing dependencies. npm is included with Node.js, while Yarn can be installed separately.
- **Code Editor:** A reliable code editor such as Visual Studio Code, Sublime Text, or Atom.

Prerequisite Knowledge:

- **JavaScript Fundamentals:** Basic understanding of JavaScript, including ES6 syntax.
- **Node.js Basics:** Familiarity with Node.js, including modules, packages, and asynchronous programming.
- **Web Development Concepts:** Basic knowledge of web development, including HTTP, RESTful APIs, and frontend frameworks (optional but beneficial).

Practical Tip: If you're new to any of these tools or concepts, consider reviewing introductory materials or tutorials to build a solid foundation before proceeding.

Setting Up Your Development Environment

Setting up your development environment correctly is crucial for a smooth learning experience. Follow these steps to get started with LangGraph.js:

Step 1: Install Node.js and npm

1. **Download Node.js:** Visit the [official Node.js website](#) and download the latest LTS (Long Term Support) version.
2. **Install Node.js:** Run the installer and follow the on-screen instructions.
3. **Verify Installation:**

bash

```
node -v
npm -v
```

These commands should display the installed versions of Node.js and npm.

Step 2: Install a Code Editor

1. **Visual Studio Code:** Download from [here](#) and install.
2. **Extensions:** Install useful extensions like ESLint, Prettier, and JavaScript (ES6) snippets to enhance your coding experience.

Step 3: Initialize a New Project

1. **Create a Project Directory:**

bash

```
mkdir langgraphjs-project
cd langgraphjs-project
```

2. **Initialize npm:**

bash

```
npm init -y
```

This command creates a package.json file with default settings.

Step 4: Install LangGraph.js

1. **Install via npm:**

bash

```
npm install langgraph.js
```

2. **Verify Installation:** Check the package.json file to ensure LangGraph.js is listed under dependencies.

Step 5: Set Up Version Control

1. **Initialize Git:**

bash

```
git init
```

2. **Create a .gitignore File:**

bash

```
echo "node_modules/" > .gitignore
```

This ensures that the node_modules directory is excluded from version control.

Step 6: Create Your First LangGraph.js File

1. **Create index.js:**

bash

```
touch index.js
```

2. **Open index.js in Your Code Editor:** Start writing your first LangGraph.js workflow (covered in the Quick Start section).

Practical Tip: Regularly commit your changes using Git to keep track of your progress and manage your code effectively.

---

4. Quick Start: Your First LangGraph.js Workflow in 15 Minutes

Ready to dive in? This quick start guide will help you set up your first LangGraph.js workflow in just 15 minutes. By the end of this section, you'll have a basic workflow up and running, providing a solid foundation for more complex projects.

4.1 Step-by-Step Setup

Follow these steps to create and run your first LangGraph.js workflow.

Step 1: Initialize Your Project

Ensure you've completed the setup steps outlined in the previous section.

Step 2: Create index.js

Open index.js in your code editor and add the following code:

javascript

```
// Import LangGraph.js
```

```javascript
const LangGraph = require('langgraph.js');

// Create a new LangGraph instance
const graph = new LangGraph();

// Define a simple agent workflow
graph.addAgent('StartAgent', async (context) => {
  console.log('Hello from StartAgent!');
  context.next();
});

graph.addAgent('EndAgent', async (context) => {
  console.log('Goodbye from EndAgent!');
});

// Define the workflow flow
graph.defineWorkflow('helloWorkflow', ['StartAgent', 'EndAgent']);

// Run the workflow
graph.run('helloWorkflow')
  .then(() => {
    console.log('Workflow completed successfully.');
  })
  .catch((error) => {
    console.error('Workflow encountered an error:', error);
  });
```

Code Explanation:
- **Import LangGraph.js:** The require statement imports the LangGraph.js library.

- **Create a LangGraph Instance:** Initializes a new LangGraph instance.
- **Define Agents:** Adds two agents, StartAgent and EndAgent, each performing a simple console log.
- **Define Workflow:** Specifies the sequence of agents in the workflow named helloWorkflow.
- **Run Workflow:** Executes the workflow and handles success or error outcomes.

Step 3: Run Your Workflow

In your terminal, execute the following command:

bash

```
node index.js
```

Expected Output:

csharp

Hello from StartAgent!

Goodbye from EndAgent!

Workflow completed successfully.

Practical Tip: Experiment by adding more agents or modifying existing ones to see how LangGraph.js handles different workflows.

Building and Running a Simple Workflow

Let's break down the workflow you just created and understand how each part works together.

1. Importing LangGraph.js:

javascript

```javascript
const LangGraph = require('langgraph.js');
```
This line imports the LangGraph.js library, making its functionalities available in your project.

2. Creating a LangGraph Instance:

javascript

```javascript
const graph = new LangGraph();
```
Here, you create a new instance of LangGraph, which will manage your agents and workflows.

3. Defining Agents:

javascript

```javascript
graph.addAgent('StartAgent', async (context) => {
  console.log('Hello from StartAgent!');
  context.next();
});

graph.addAgent('EndAgent', async (context) => {
  console.log('Goodbye from EndAgent!');
});
```

- **StartAgent:** Logs a greeting message and proceeds to the next agent using context.next().
- **EndAgent:** Logs a farewell message. Since there are no subsequent agents, the workflow concludes here.

4. Defining the Workflow:

javascript

```javascript
graph.defineWorkflow('helloWorkflow', ['StartAgent', 'EndAgent']);
```

This line defines a workflow named helloWorkflow consisting of StartAgent followed by EndAgent.

5. Running the Workflow:

javascript

```javascript
graph.run('helloWorkflow')
  .then(() => {
    console.log('Workflow completed successfully.');
  })
  .catch((error) => {
    console.error('Workflow encountered an error:', error);
  });
```

- **graph.run('helloWorkflow'):** Initiates the execution of the defined workflow.
- **.then(...):** Logs a success message upon successful completion.
- **.catch(...):** Handles any errors that occur during workflow execution.

Practical Example: Consider extending this simple workflow by adding an agent that processes data or interacts with an external API, demonstrating how workflows can be built incrementally.

Immediate Debugging and Logging

Effective debugging and logging are essential for developing reliable workflows. LangGraph.js provides built-in mechanisms to help you monitor and troubleshoot your workflows.

Enhanced Logging: To gain more insights into your workflow's execution, you can add detailed logging at various stages.

Example: Adding Detailed Logs

javascript

```javascript
// Import LangGraph.js
const LangGraph = require('langgraph.js');

// Create a new LangGraph instance with logging enabled
const graph = new LangGraph({
  logging: true, // Enable detailed logging
});

// Define a simple agent workflow with additional logs
graph.addAgent('StartAgent', async (context) => {
  console.log('[StartAgent] Initiating workflow.');
  context.next();
});

graph.addAgent('MiddleAgent', async (context) => {
  console.log('[MiddleAgent] Processing data...');
  // Simulate data processing
  context.data = { message: 'Data processed successfully.' };
  context.next();
});

graph.addAgent('EndAgent', async (context) => {
  console.log('[EndAgent] Finalizing workflow.');
  console.log(`[EndAgent] Message: ${context.data.message}`);
});

// Define the workflow flow
graph.defineWorkflow('detailedWorkflow', ['StartAgent', 'MiddleAgent', 'EndAgent']);

// Run the workflow
```

```
graph.run('detailedWorkflow')
  .then(() => {
    console.log('Workflow completed successfully.');
  })
  .catch((error) => {
    console.error('Workflow encountered an error:', error);
  });
```

Code Explanation:

- **Enable Logging:** By passing { logging: true } when creating the LangGraph instance, detailed logs are generated during workflow execution.

- **MiddleAgent:** An additional agent that simulates data processing and stores the result in context.data.

- **Enhanced Logs:** Each agent logs its specific actions, providing a clear trace of the workflow's progression.

Expected Output:

csharp

[StartAgent] Initiating workflow.

[MiddleAgent] Processing data...

[EndAgent] Finalizing workflow.

[EndAgent] Message: Data processed successfully.

Workflow completed successfully.

Error Handling: Implementing robust error handling ensures your workflows can gracefully manage unexpected issues.

Example: Handling Errors Gracefully

javascript

```
// Define an agent that may throw an error
```

```javascript
graph.addAgent('ErrorAgent', async (context) => {
  console.log('[ErrorAgent] Attempting risky operation.');
  try {
    // Simulate an error
    throw new Error('Simulated error in ErrorAgent.');
  } catch (error) {
    console.error('[ErrorAgent] Caught an error:', error.message);
    // Decide whether to continue or halt the workflow
    context.stop(); // Halts the workflow
  }
});

// Define a workflow with an error-prone agent
graph.defineWorkflow('errorHandlingWorkflow', ['StartAgent', 'ErrorAgent', 'EndAgent']);

// Run the workflow
graph.run('errorHandlingWorkflow')
  .then(() => {
    console.log('Workflow completed successfully.');
  })
  .catch((error) => {
    console.error('Workflow encountered an error:', error);
  });
```

Code Explanation:

- **ErrorAgent:** An agent designed to simulate an error during execution.
- **Try-Catch Block:** Catches the simulated error and logs it.
- **context.stop():** Halts the workflow upon encountering an error, preventing subsequent agents from executing.

Expected Output:

csharp

[StartAgent] Initiating workflow.

[ErrorAgent] Attempting risky operation.

[ErrorAgent] Caught an error: Simulated error in ErrorAgent.

Workflow completed successfully.

Note: Although the workflow stops after the error, the .then() block is still executed. To differentiate between successful and halted executions, consider modifying the workflow runner to handle stopped workflows separately.

Best Practices for Debugging and Logging:

- **Consistent Logging:** Use consistent log messages to make it easier to trace and debug workflows.
- **Granular Logs:** Include detailed logs within agents to monitor specific actions and data transformations.
- **Error Handling Strategies:** Implement strategies like retries, fallbacks, and circuit breakers to manage errors effectively.

Practical Tip: Utilize logging libraries like Winston or Bunyan for more advanced logging capabilities, such as log levels, formatting, and persistent storage.

This introduction has laid the groundwork for your journey with LangGraph.js. We've explored the evolution and significance of agent workflows, identified the target audience for this book, outlined how to effectively utilize the guide, and provided a quick start to get you hands-on with your first LangGraph.js workflow. As you proceed through the chapters, you'll build upon these foundational concepts, delving deeper into the capabilities of LangGraph.js and applying them to real-world scenarios.

Remember, the key to mastering LangGraph.js lies in understanding both the theoretical underpinnings and the practical applications. This book is designed to provide a balanced approach, ensuring you gain the skills and confidence needed to build sophisticated multi-agent systems in your projects.

Let's embark on this exciting journey to harness the power of LangGraph.js and revolutionize the way you build and manage agent workflows!

Chapter 1: Getting Started with LangGraph.js

In this chapter, we'll introduce you to the fundamental concepts of agent workflows and multi-agent systems, guide you through setting up LangGraph.js in your development environment, and help you build your first simple agent workflow. By the end of this chapter, you'll have a solid foundation to continue your journey with LangGraph.js.

1.1 Understanding Agent Workflows and Multi-Agent Systems

To effectively use LangGraph.js, it's essential to grasp the core concepts and terminology related to agent workflows and multi-agent systems. This section will break down these concepts and showcase their real-world applications.

1.1.1 Core Concepts and Terminology

Agent Workflows: An agent workflow is a sequence of tasks or operations performed by autonomous entities called agents. These workflows automate processes, enabling systems to perform complex tasks without human intervention.

Multi-Agent Systems (MAS): A multi-agent system consists of multiple interacting agents, each with specific roles and responsibilities. These agents collaborate to achieve common goals, handle large-scale tasks, and adapt to changing environments.

Key Terminology:

Term	Definition
Agent	An autonomous entity capable of performing tasks and making decisions.
Workflow	A sequence of tasks or operations designed to accomplish a specific objective.
Orchestration	The management and coordination of multiple agents to execute workflows.
Concurrency	The ability of agents to perform tasks simultaneously.
Context	The state or data shared among agents during workflow execution.
Scalability	The capacity to handle increasing workloads by adding more agents or resources.

Core Concepts:

1. **Autonomy:** Agents operate independently, making decisions based on predefined rules or learned behaviors.
2. **Communication:** Agents interact through messaging or shared contexts to coordinate tasks.
3. **Collaboration:** Agents work together to achieve goals that are beyond the capability of a single agent.
4. **Adaptability:** Agents can adjust their actions based on feedback and changing conditions.

Example Scenario: Imagine an online retail platform where multiple agents handle different aspects of order processing:

- **Inventory Agent:** Monitors stock levels and updates inventory.

- **Payment Agent:** Processes customer payments securely.
- **Shipping Agent:** Arranges for product delivery to customers.
- **Notification Agent:** Sends order confirmations and shipping updates to customers.

Each agent operates autonomously but collaborates to ensure a seamless order processing experience.

1.1.2 Real-World Applications

Understanding how agent workflows and multi-agent systems are applied in the real world can provide valuable insights into their potential. Here are some notable applications:

1. E-Commerce:

- **Automated Inventory Management:** Agents track stock levels, reorder products, and manage suppliers.
- **Personalized Recommendations:** Agents analyze customer behavior to suggest products tailored to individual preferences.

2. Financial Services:

- **Fraud Detection:** Agents monitor transactions in real-time to identify and flag suspicious activities.
- **Automated Trading:** Agents execute trades based on market analysis and predefined strategies.

3. Healthcare:

- **Patient Monitoring:** Agents collect and analyze patient data to provide timely alerts to healthcare professionals.
- **Appointment Scheduling:** Agents manage and optimize appointment bookings, reducing wait times and improving patient experience.

4. Smart Homes:

- **Energy Management:** Agents control lighting, heating, and cooling systems to optimize energy usage.

- **Security Systems:** Agents monitor and respond to security threats, such as unauthorized access or unusual activities.

5. **AI-Powered Applications:**
    - **Chatbots:** Intelligent agents interact with users, providing customer support and handling inquiries.
    - **Natural Language Processing (NLP):** Agents process and understand human language to perform tasks like translation, sentiment analysis, and content generation.

Case Study: Automated Customer Support A telecommunications company uses a multi-agent system to manage customer support:

- **Inquiry Agent:** Handles general customer inquiries and provides information.
- **Troubleshooting Agent:** Assists customers in diagnosing and resolving technical issues.
- **Feedback Agent:** Collects and analyzes customer feedback to improve services.

This system enhances customer satisfaction by providing quick and accurate responses while reducing the workload on human support staff.

1.2 Setting Up LangGraph.js

Before diving into building agent workflows, you need to set up LangGraph.js in your development environment. This section will guide you through installing LangGraph.js using npm or yarn and help you understand its dependencies.

1.2.1 Installing LangGraph.js via npm/yarn

LangGraph.js is a JavaScript library that can be easily integrated into your Node.js projects using npm or yarn. Follow these steps to install LangGraph.js:

Step 1: Initialize a New Node.js Project

If you haven't already, create a new directory for your project and initialize it with npm:

bash

```
mkdir langgraphjs-project
cd langgraphjs-project
npm init -y
```

Explanation:

- mkdir langgraphjs-project: Creates a new directory named langgraphjs-project.
- cd langgraphjs-project: Navigates into the newly created directory.
- npm init -y: Initializes a new Node.js project with default settings, creating a package.json file.

Step 2: Install LangGraph.js

You can install LangGraph.js using either npm or yarn. Choose the package manager you're most comfortable with.

Using npm:

bash

```
npm install langgraph.js
```

Using yarn:

bash

```
yarn add langgraph.js
```

Explanation:

- npm install langgraph.js or yarn add langgraph.js: Downloads and installs the LangGraph.js library along with its dependencies into your project.

Step 3: Verify Installation

After installation, verify that LangGraph.js is listed in your package.json under dependencies.

Example package.json:

json

```
{
  "name": "langgraphjs-project",
  "version": "1.0.0",
  "description": "A project to explore LangGraph.js",
  "main": "index.js",
  "dependencies": {
    "langgraph.js": "^1.2.3"
  },
  "devDependencies": {},
  "scripts": {
    "start": "node index.js"
  },
  "author": "",
  "license": "ISC"
}
```

Note: The version number (^1.2.3) may vary based on the latest release of LangGraph.js.

1.2.2 Understanding Dependencies

LangGraph.js relies on several dependencies to function correctly. Understanding these dependencies helps you manage and troubleshoot your project effectively.

Core Dependencies:

Dependency	Purpose
Node.js	Provides the runtime environment for executing JS code.
npm/yarn	Package managers used to install and manage dependencies.
LangGraph.js	The main library for building agent workflows and multi-agent systems.

Additional Dependencies:

Depending on your project's requirements, you might need to install additional libraries or tools. Some common dependencies include:

Dependency Purpose

Express.js	A web framework for building backend applications.
Socket.io	Enables real-time, bidirectional communication between clients and servers.
Winston	A logging library for Node.js applications.
Dotenv	Loads environment variables from a .env file into process.env.

Installing Additional Dependencies:

To install any of these dependencies, use npm or yarn. For example, to install Express.js and Socket.io using npm:

bash

```
npm install express socket.io
```

Explanation:

- express: A minimalist web framework for Node.js.
- socket.io: A library for real-time web applications, enabling real-time communication between the client and server.

Practical Tip: Only install the dependencies you need for your project to keep your application lightweight and manageable.

Dependency Management Best Practices:

- **Version Control:** Specify exact version numbers in your package.json to ensure consistency across different environments.
- **Regular Updates:** Keep your dependencies updated to benefit from the latest features, performance improvements, and security patches.
- **Use .gitignore:** Exclude node_modules from your version control system by adding it to your .gitignore file.

2.3 Your First Agent Workflow

Now that LangGraph.js is set up, it's time to build your first simple agent workflow. This section will guide you through creating a "Hello, Agent" example and provide a quick exercise to reinforce your understanding.

2.3.1 Building a Simple "Hello, Agent" Example

Let's create a basic workflow with two agents that greet the user. This simple example will help you understand how agents are defined, how workflows are structured, and how to run them using LangGraph.js.

Step 1: Create index.js

In your project directory, create a file named index.js:

bash

```
touch index.js
```

Step 2: Write the Workflow Code

Open index.js in your code editor and add the following code:

javascript

```javascript
// Import LangGraph.js
const LangGraph = require('langgraph.js');

// Create a new LangGraph instance
const graph = new LangGraph();

// Define the StartAgent
graph.addAgent('StartAgent', async (context) => {
  console.log('Hello from StartAgent!');
  context.next(); // Proceed to the next agent
});

// Define the EndAgent
graph.addAgent('EndAgent', async (context) => {
  console.log('Goodbye from EndAgent!');
});

// Define the workflow sequence
graph.defineWorkflow('helloWorkflow', ['StartAgent', 'EndAgent']);

// Run the workflow
graph.run('helloWorkflow')
  .then(() => {
    console.log('Workflow completed successfully.');
  })
  .catch((error) => {
    console.error('Workflow encountered an error:', error);
  });
```

Code Explanation:
1. **Import LangGraph.js:**

javascript

```javascript
const LangGraph = require('langgraph.js');
```
This line imports the LangGraph.js library, making its functionalities available in your project.

2. **Create a LangGraph Instance:**

javascript

```javascript
const graph = new LangGraph();
```
Initializes a new instance of LangGraph, which will manage your agents and workflows.

3. **Define the StartAgent:**

javascript

```javascript
graph.addAgent('StartAgent', async (context) => {
  console.log('Hello from StartAgent!');
  context.next(); // Proceed to the next agent
});
```

- **Agent Name:** StartAgent
- **Function:** Logs a greeting message and calls context.next() to move to the next agent in the workflow.

4. **Define the EndAgent:**

javascript

```javascript
graph.addAgent('EndAgent', async (context) => {
  console.log('Goodbye from EndAgent!');
});
```

- **Agent Name:** EndAgent

- **Function:** Logs a farewell message. Since there are no further agents, the workflow ends here.

5. **Define the Workflow Sequence:**

javascript

```
graph.defineWorkflow('helloWorkflow', ['StartAgent', 'EndAgent']);
```

- **Workflow Name:** helloWorkflow
- **Sequence:** Specifies that StartAgent will execute first, followed by EndAgent.

6. **Run the Workflow:**

javascript

```
graph.run('helloWorkflow')
  .then(() => {
    console.log('Workflow completed successfully.');
  })
  .catch((error) => {
    console.error('Workflow encountered an error:', error);
  });
```

- **Execution:** Initiates the workflow named helloWorkflow.
- **Success Handler:** Logs a success message upon successful completion.
- **Error Handler:** Catches and logs any errors that occur during workflow execution.

Step 3: Execute the Workflow

In your terminal, run the following command to execute the workflow:

bash

```
node index.js
```

Expected Output:

csharp

```
Hello from StartAgent!
Goodbye from EndAgent!
Workflow completed successfully.
```

Code Snippet with Comments:

javascript

```
// Import LangGraph.js
const LangGraph = require('langgraph.js');

// Create a new LangGraph instance
const graph = new LangGraph();

// Define the StartAgent
graph.addAgent('StartAgent', async (context) => {
  console.log('Hello from StartAgent!'); // Agent logs a greeting message
  context.next(); // Proceed to the next agent in the workflow
});

// Define the EndAgent
```

```
graph.addAgent('EndAgent', async (context) => {
  console.log('Goodbye from EndAgent!'); // Agent logs a farewell message
});

// Define the workflow sequence
graph.defineWorkflow('helloWorkflow', ['StartAgent',
'EndAgent']); // Specifies the order of agent execution

// Run the workflow
graph.run('helloWorkflow') // Initiates the workflow
  .then(() => {
    console.log('Workflow completed successfully.'); // Logs success message
  })
  .catch((error) => {
    console.error('Workflow encountered an error:', error);
// Logs any errors
  });
```

1.3.2 Quick Exercise: Creating a Basic Workflow in 10 Steps

To reinforce your understanding of building agent workflows with LangGraph.js, complete this quick exercise. Follow the 10 steps below to create a basic workflow that includes three agents: StartAgent, MiddleAgent, and EndAgent.

Objective: Build a workflow where:

1. StartAgent initiates the process.
2. MiddleAgent processes some data.
3. EndAgent concludes the workflow.

Steps:

1. **Initialize a New Node.js Project:**

bash

```
mkdir basic-workflow
cd basic-workflow
npm init -y
```

2. **Install LangGraph.js:**

bash

```
npm install langgraph.js
```

3. **Create index.js:**

bash

```
touch index.js
```

4. **Import LangGraph.js in index.js:**

javascript

```
const LangGraph = require('langgraph.js');
```

5. **Create a LangGraph Instance:**

javascript

```
const graph = new LangGraph();
```

6. **Define StartAgent:**

javascript

```
graph.addAgent('StartAgent', async (context) => {
  console.log('StartAgent: Beginning the workflow.');
  context.next();
```

});

7. **Define MiddleAgent:**

javascript

```
graph.addAgent('MiddleAgent', async (context) => {
  console.log('MiddleAgent: Processing data...');
  context.data = { processed: true };
  context.next();
});
```

8. **Define EndAgent:**

javascript

```
graph.addAgent('EndAgent', async (context) => {
  console.log('EndAgent: Workflow has been completed.');
  console.log('Processed Data:', context.data);
});
```

9. **Define the Workflow Sequence:**

javascript

```
graph.defineWorkflow('basicWorkflow', ['StartAgent', 'MiddleAgent', 'EndAgent']);
```

10. **Run the Workflow and Handle Outcomes:**

javascript

```
graph.run('basicWorkflow')
  .then(() => {
    console.log('Basic Workflow executed successfully.');
  })
```

```javascript
    .catch((error) => {
      console.error('Error executing Basic Workflow:', error);
    });
```

Complete index.js Code:

javascript

```javascript
// Import LangGraph.js
const LangGraph = require('langgraph.js');

// Create a new LangGraph instance
const graph = new LangGraph();

// Define StartAgent
graph.addAgent('StartAgent', async (context) => {
  console.log('StartAgent: Beginning the workflow.');
  context.next(); // Proceed to MiddleAgent
});

// Define MiddleAgent
graph.addAgent('MiddleAgent', async (context) => {
  console.log('MiddleAgent: Processing data...');
  context.data = { processed: true }; // Store processed data in context
  context.next(); // Proceed to EndAgent
});

// Define EndAgent
graph.addAgent('EndAgent', async (context) => {
  console.log('EndAgent: Workflow has been completed.');
```

```
    console.log('Processed Data:', context.data); // Access and
display processed data
});

// Define the workflow sequence
graph.defineWorkflow('basicWorkflow', ['StartAgent',
'MiddleAgent', 'EndAgent']);

// Run the workflow
graph.run('basicWorkflow')
  .then(() => {
    console.log('Basic Workflow executed successfully.');
  })
  .catch((error) => {
    console.error('Error executing Basic Workflow:', error);
  });
```

Step 11: Execute the Workflow

Run the following command in your terminal:

bash

```
node index.js
```

Expected Output:

yaml

StartAgent: Beginning the workflow.

MiddleAgent: Processing data...

EndAgent: Workflow has been completed.

Processed Data: { processed: true }

Basic Workflow executed successfully.

Explanation of the Workflow:

1. **StartAgent:** Initiates the workflow by logging a starting message and calls context.next() to move to the next agent.

2. **MiddleAgent:** Processes data by setting context.data and logs a processing message before calling context.next() to proceed.

3. **EndAgent:** Concludes the workflow by logging a completion message and accessing the processed data from context.data.

Practical Tip: Experiment by adding more agents or modifying existing ones to see how LangGraph.js manages different workflows and data flows.

Summary

In Chapter 1, we've laid the groundwork for understanding agent workflows and multi-agent systems, set up LangGraph.js in your development environment, and built your first simple agent workflow. These foundational steps are crucial as you continue to explore more complex and powerful applications of LangGraph.js in subsequent chapters.

Key Takeaways:

- **Agent Workflows:** Automate tasks through autonomous agents working in sequence or parallel.

- **Multi-Agent Systems:** Enhance system capabilities by enabling multiple agents to collaborate and adapt.

- **LangGraph.js Setup:** Easy installation via npm or yarn, with manageable dependencies.

- **First Workflow:** A simple example demonstrates how to define and run a workflow using LangGraph.js.

As you move forward, you'll delve deeper into more advanced concepts, integrations, and real-world applications, equipping you with the skills to build sophisticated multi-agent systems using LangGraph.js.

Chapter 2: Core Concepts of LangGraph.js

In this chapter, we'll dive deep into the foundational concepts that underpin LangGraph.js. Understanding these core concepts is crucial for designing effective agent workflows and multi-agent systems. We'll explore what agents are, how to design simple workflows, the structure of nodes and graphs, and the importance of asynchronous processing in managing concurrency. By the end of this chapter, you'll be equipped with the knowledge to create robust and efficient workflows using LangGraph.js.

2.1 Agents and Workflows

Agents are the building blocks of workflows in LangGraph.js. They perform specific tasks, interact with other agents, and collectively drive the workflow towards its objectives. Understanding the nature of agents and how to design workflows is essential for leveraging the full potential of LangGraph.js.

2.1.1 What are Agents?

Agents are autonomous entities within LangGraph.js that perform discrete tasks as part of a larger workflow. Each agent operates independently but can communicate and collaborate with other agents to achieve complex goals. Agents can be thought of as specialized workers, each responsible for a particular aspect of the workflow.

Key Characteristics of Agents:

1. **Autonomy:** Agents operate independently, making decisions based on their programming and the data they process.

2. **Specialization:** Each agent is designed to perform specific tasks, allowing for modular and organized workflows.

3. **Communication:** Agents can send and receive messages or share data with other agents to coordinate actions.

4. **State Management:** Agents can maintain state information, enabling them to perform tasks that require context or historical data.

Example Scenario: Consider a simple data processing workflow where data is fetched from an API, processed, and then stored in a database. This workflow can be broken down into three agents:

- **FetcherAgent:** Fetches data from the API.
- **ProcessorAgent:** Processes the fetched data.
- **StorageAgent:** Stores the processed data in the database.

Each agent handles its specific task, and together, they form a cohesive workflow.

2.1.2 Designing Simple Workflows

Designing workflows involves defining the sequence and interaction of agents to accomplish a specific objective. A well-designed workflow ensures that tasks are executed efficiently, errors are handled gracefully, and the system remains scalable and maintainable.

Steps to Design a Simple Workflow:

1. **Define the Objective:**
   - Clearly articulate what the workflow is intended to achieve.
   - Example: Automate the process of fetching, processing, and storing data from an external API.

2. **Identify the Required Agents:**
   - Determine the tasks that need to be performed and assign each task to an agent.
   - Example:
     - **FetcherAgent:** Fetch data from the API.
     - **ProcessorAgent:** Process the fetched data.
     - **StorageAgent:** Store the processed data.

3. **Establish the Sequence:**

- Determine the order in which agents should execute their tasks.
- Example: FetcherAgent → ProcessorAgent → StorageAgent.

4. **Define Communication and Data Flow:**
   - Specify how agents will pass data and signals to each other.
   - Example: FetcherAgent sends fetched data to ProcessorAgent; ProcessorAgent sends processed data to StorageAgent.

5. **Implement Error Handling:**
   - Design mechanisms to handle potential errors at each stage of the workflow.
   - Example: If FetcherAgent fails to fetch data, trigger a retry mechanism or alert the system.

6. **Test and Refine:**
   - Run the workflow to identify and fix any issues.
   - Example: Verify that data flows correctly between agents and that errors are handled as expected.

Practical Example: Let's design a simple workflow to automate email sending based on user sign-ups:

- **SignupAgent:** Handles user sign-up and triggers the workflow.
- **EmailAgent:** Sends a welcome email to the new user.
- **LoggingAgent:** Logs the email sending activity for record-keeping.

Workflow Sequence:

1. **SignupAgent** receives a new user sign-up.
2. **EmailAgent** sends a welcome email to the user.

3. **LoggingAgent** records the email sending activity.

Best Practices for Designing Workflows:

- **Modularity:** Keep agents focused on single responsibilities to enhance reusability and maintainability.

- **Scalability:** Design workflows that can handle increased load by adding more agents or distributing tasks.

- **Error Resilience:** Implement robust error handling to ensure the workflow can recover from failures without significant disruptions.

- **Clear Communication:** Define clear protocols for how agents communicate and share data to avoid misunderstandings and bottlenecks.

2.2 Nodes and Graphs

In LangGraph.js, workflows are structured as graphs composed of nodes and edges. Understanding how nodes and edges function is vital for designing effective workflows.

2.2.1 Understanding Node Structures

Nodes are the fundamental units in a LangGraph.js workflow graph. Each node represents an agent that performs a specific task. Nodes can be connected to form complex workflows, enabling the execution of multiple tasks in a coordinated manner.

Components of a Node:

1. **Identifier:** A unique name or ID that distinguishes the node within the graph.

2. **Agent Function:** The function or logic that the agent executes.

3. **Input Ports:** Points where the node receives data or signals from other nodes.

4. **Output Ports:** Points where the node sends data or signals to other nodes.

Node Structure Example:

javascript

```
graph.addAgent('FetcherAgent', async (context) => {
  // Agent logic here
});
```

Explanation:

- **'FetcherAgent':** The unique identifier for the node.
- **Agent Function:** An asynchronous function that defines what FetcherAgent does when executed.

Types of Nodes:

1. **Action Nodes:** Perform specific actions such as fetching data, processing information, or sending notifications.
2. **Decision Nodes:** Make decisions based on certain conditions, directing the workflow accordingly.
3. **End Nodes:** Signify the completion of the workflow.

2.2.2 The Role of Edges in Workflows

Edges are the connections between nodes in a graph. They define the flow of data and control between agents, determining the sequence and interaction within the workflow.

Functions of Edges:

1. **Data Transfer:** Carry data from one agent to another, enabling agents to use the output of previous agents as their input.
2. **Control Flow:** Direct the execution order of agents, determining which agent runs next based on conditions or triggers.
3. **Synchronization:** Coordinate the timing of agent executions, ensuring that agents run in the correct sequence.

Edge Structure Example:

javascript

```
graph.defineWorkflow('dataProcessingWorkflow',
['FetcherAgent', 'ProcessorAgent', 'StorageAgent']);
```

Explanation:

- **'dataProcessingWorkflow':** The name of the workflow graph.
- **['FetcherAgent', 'ProcessorAgent', 'StorageAgent']:** The sequence of nodes connected by edges, defining the order of agent execution.

Types of Edges:

1. **Sequential Edges:** Define a linear sequence where each agent runs one after the other.
2. **Parallel Edges:** Allow multiple agents to run simultaneously, enhancing workflow efficiency.
3. **Conditional Edges:** Direct the workflow based on specific conditions or data values, enabling dynamic and responsive workflows.

Best Practices for Using Nodes and Edges:

- **Clear Naming:** Use descriptive names for nodes to easily identify their roles within the workflow.
- **Minimal Dependencies:** Design workflows with minimal interdependencies between agents to enhance flexibility and reduce complexity.
- **Consistent Data Formats:** Ensure that data passed between agents follows consistent formats to prevent errors and facilitate smooth data flow.
- **Documentation:** Maintain clear documentation of node structures and edge connections to aid in workflow maintenance and scalability.

2.3 Asynchronous Processing

As workflows become more complex, managing concurrency and ensuring efficient execution of multiple tasks simultaneously becomes crucial. LangGraph.js leverages asynchronous processing to handle such scenarios effectively.

2.3.1 Managing Concurrency in Multi-Agent Systems

Concurrency refers to the ability of a system to execute multiple tasks or processes simultaneously. In multi-agent systems, managing concurrency ensures that agents can perform their tasks without blocking each other, leading to improved performance and responsiveness.

Challenges in Managing Concurrency:

1. **Resource Contention:** Multiple agents may compete for the same resources, leading to bottlenecks.

2. **Data Consistency:** Ensuring that concurrent tasks do not lead to inconsistent data states.

3. **Deadlocks:** Situations where agents are waiting indefinitely for resources held by each other, halting workflow progress.

Strategies for Managing Concurrency:

1. **Asynchronous Execution:** Use asynchronous programming paradigms to allow agents to run independently without waiting for each other to complete.

2. **Task Scheduling:** Implement scheduling mechanisms to prioritize and manage the execution order of agents based on their importance and resource requirements.

3. **Resource Allocation:** Allocate dedicated resources to critical agents to prevent resource contention and ensure smooth execution.

4. **Concurrency Control:** Use locks, semaphores, or other concurrency control mechanisms to manage access to shared resources and maintain data consistency.

Practical Example: Imagine a workflow where multiple agents fetch data from different APIs simultaneously. By managing concurrency, these agents can run in parallel, reducing the overall time required to gather data.

2.3.2 Promises and Callbacks in LangGraph.js

LangGraph.js utilizes JavaScript's asynchronous features, such as **Promises** and **Callbacks**, to manage the execution of agents and handle asynchronous operations within workflows.

Promises: A Promise represents a value that may be available now, in the future, or never. Promises provide a cleaner and more manageable way to handle asynchronous operations compared to traditional callbacks.

Basic Promise Structure:

javascript

```javascript
const fetchData = () => {
  return new Promise((resolve, reject) => {
    // Asynchronous operation
    if (success) {
      resolve(data);
    } else {
      reject(error);
    }
  });
};

fetchData()
  .then((data) => {
    console.log('Data fetched:', data);
  })
  .catch((error) => {
```

```
    console.error('Error fetching data:', error);
  });
```

Callbacks: Callbacks are functions passed as arguments to other functions, which are invoked after an asynchronous operation completes. While effective, callbacks can lead to callback hell if not managed properly.

Basic Callback Structure:

javascript

```
const fetchData = (callback) => {
  // Asynchronous operation
  if (success) {
    callback(null, data);
  } else {
    callback(error);
  }
};

fetchData((error, data) => {
  if (error) {
    console.error('Error fetching data:', error);
  } else {
    console.log('Data fetched:', data);
  }
});
```

Using Promises in LangGraph.js:

LangGraph.js agents can return Promises to handle asynchronous tasks, allowing workflows to wait for agents to complete their tasks before proceeding.

Example: Asynchronous Agent Using Promises

javascript

```javascript
graph.addAgent('AsyncAgent', async (context) => {
  try {
    const data = await fetchDataFromAPI();
    console.log('AsyncAgent received data:', data);
    context.next();
  } catch (error) {
    console.error('AsyncAgent encountered an error:', error);
    context.stop(); // Halts the workflow on error
  }
});
```

Explanation:

- **async Function:** Declares the agent function as asynchronous.
- **await fetchDataFromAPI():** Waits for the Promise returned by fetchDataFromAPI() to resolve before proceeding.
- **Error Handling:** Uses try-catch blocks to handle any errors that occur during the asynchronous operation.

Best Practices:

- **Use Promises Over Callbacks:** Promises provide better readability and easier error handling.
- **Handle Errors Gracefully:** Always include error handling within asynchronous agents to prevent workflow disruptions.
- **Chain Promises Carefully:** Ensure that Promises are properly chained to maintain the correct sequence of agent executions.

2.3.3 Example: A Concurrent Data Processing Workflow

Let's create an example workflow that demonstrates concurrent data processing using asynchronous agents. This workflow will fetch data from multiple sources simultaneously, process the data, and then store the results.

Workflow Overview:

1. **FetcherAgent1:** Fetches data from Source A.
2. **FetcherAgent2:** Fetches data from Source B.
3. **ProcessorAgent:** Processes the combined data from both sources.
4. **StorageAgent:** Stores the processed data.

Step-by-Step Implementation:

1. **Initialize the Project:**

Ensure you have a Node.js project set up with LangGraph.js installed.

bash

```
mkdir concurrent-workflow
cd concurrent-workflow
npm init -y
npm install langgraph.js axios
```

Explanation:

- **axios:** A promise-based HTTP client for making API requests.

2. **Create index.js:**

bash

```
touch index.js
```

3. **Write the Workflow Code:**

Open index.js in your code editor and add the following code:

```javascript
// Import LangGraph.js and Axios
const LangGraph = require('langgraph.js');
const axios = require('axios');

// Create a new LangGraph instance
const graph = new LangGraph();

// Define FetcherAgent1: Fetches data from Source A
graph.addAgent('FetcherAgent1', async (context) => {
  try {
    const response = await axios.get('https://api.sourcea.com/data');
    context.data.sourceA = response.data;
    console.log('FetcherAgent1: Data fetched from Source A.');
    context.next();
  } catch (error) {
    console.error('FetcherAgent1 encountered an error:', error.message);
    context.stop(); // Halts the workflow on error
  }
});

// Define FetcherAgent2: Fetches data from Source B
graph.addAgent('FetcherAgent2', async (context) => {
  try {
    const response = await axios.get('https://api.sourceb.com/data');
    context.data.sourceB = response.data;
```

```
    console.log('FetcherAgent2: Data fetched from Source B.');
    context.next();
  } catch (error) {
    console.error('FetcherAgent2 encountered an error:', error.message);
    context.stop(); // Halts the workflow on error
  }
});

// Define ProcessorAgent: Processes the combined data
graph.addAgent('ProcessorAgent', async (context) => {
  try {
    const combinedData = { ...context.data.sourceA, ...context.data.sourceB };
    context.data.processed = processData(combinedData);
    console.log('ProcessorAgent: Data processed successfully.');
    context.next();
  } catch (error) {
    console.error('ProcessorAgent encountered an error:', error.message);
    context.stop(); // Halts the workflow on error
  }
});

// Define StorageAgent: Stores the processed data
graph.addAgent('StorageAgent', async (context) => {
  try {
    await storeData(context.data.processed);
    console.log('StorageAgent: Data stored successfully.');
```

```
    context.next();
  } catch (error) {
    console.error('StorageAgent encountered an error:',
error.message);
    context.stop(); // Halts the workflow on error
  }
});

// Define the workflow sequence
graph.defineWorkflow('concurrentDataProcessing', [
  'FetcherAgent1',
  'FetcherAgent2',
  'ProcessorAgent',
  'StorageAgent',
]);

// Run the workflow
graph
  .run('concurrentDataProcessing')
  .then(() => {
    console.log('Concurrent Data Processing Workflow completed successfully.');
  })
  .catch((error) => {
    console.error('Concurrent Data Processing Workflow encountered an error:', error);
  });

// Helper function to process data
function processData(data) {
  // Example data processing logic
```

```
  return {
    combined: data,
    timestamp: new Date(),
  };
}

// Helper function to store data
async function storeData(processedData) {
  // Example storage logic (e.g., saving to a database)
  // For demonstration, we'll just log the data
  console.log('Storing Data:', processedData);
}
```

4. **Code Explanation:**
    - **Importing Libraries:**

javascript

```
const LangGraph = require('langgraph.js');
const axios = require('axios');
```
Imports LangGraph.js for workflow management and Axios for making HTTP requests.

   - **Creating LangGraph Instance:**

javascript

```
const graph = new LangGraph();
```
Initializes a new LangGraph instance to manage agents and workflows.

   - **Defining Agents:**
        - **FetcherAgent1 and FetcherAgent2:** These agents fetch data from two different sources concurrently. They store the fetched data in

context.data.sourceA and context.data.sourceB respectively.

- **ProcessorAgent:** Combines and processes the data fetched by the previous agents. The processed data is stored in context.data.processed.
- **StorageAgent:** Stores the processed data. In this example, it simply logs the data, but it can be extended to store data in a database or other storage systems.

- **Defining the Workflow:**

javascript

```
graph.defineWorkflow('concurrentDataProcessing', [
  'FetcherAgent1',
  'FetcherAgent2',
  'ProcessorAgent',
  'StorageAgent',
]);
```

Specifies the sequence of agents in the workflow. Both FetcherAgent1 and FetcherAgent2 run concurrently before ProcessorAgent and StorageAgent execute sequentially.

- **Running the Workflow:**

javascript

```
graph
  .run('concurrentDataProcessing')
  .then(() => {
    console.log('Concurrent Data Processing Workflow completed successfully.');
  })
```

```
    .catch((error) => {
      console.error('Concurrent Data Processing Workflow
encountered an error:', error);
    });
```

Initiates the workflow and handles success or error outcomes.

- **Helper Functions:**
    - **processData:** Processes the combined data. In this example, it merges the data and adds a timestamp.
    - **storeData:** Stores the processed data. Currently, it logs the data but can be expanded to perform actual storage operations.

5. **Execute the Workflow:**

Run the workflow using the following command in your terminal:

bash

```
node index.js
```

6. **Expected Output:**

yaml

```
FetcherAgent1: Data fetched from Source A.
FetcherAgent2: Data fetched from Source B.
ProcessorAgent: Data processed successfully.
Storing Data: { combined: { /* data from Source A and B */ }, timestamp: 2024-12-18T12:34:56.789Z }
StorageAgent: Data stored successfully.
```

Concurrent Data Processing Workflow completed successfully.

Notes:

- **Concurrency Handling:** LangGraph.js manages the concurrent execution of FetcherAgent1 and FetcherAgent2, allowing both agents to run simultaneously without blocking each other.

- **Error Handling:** Each agent includes try-catch blocks to handle errors gracefully. If an agent encounters an error, it logs the error and halts the workflow using context.stop().

- **Data Flow:** Data is passed between agents using the context object, ensuring that each agent has access to the necessary information for its tasks.

Best Practices Illustrated:

- **Modular Agent Design:** Each agent is responsible for a specific task, promoting reusability and maintainability.

- **Asynchronous Operations:** Leveraging Promises and async/await ensures efficient handling of asynchronous tasks.

- **Robust Error Handling:** Implementing error handling within each agent prevents workflow failures and ensures that issues are logged and managed appropriately.

2.4 Mini-Project: Creating a Workflow to Fetch and Process API Data

To solidify your understanding of the core concepts discussed in this chapter, let's embark on a mini-project. In this project, you'll create a workflow that fetches data from an external API, processes the data, and stores the results. This hands-on exercise will help you apply the concepts of agents, nodes, graphs, and asynchronous processing in a practical scenario.

Project Overview:

- **Objective:** Build a workflow that fetches weather data from a public API, processes the data to extract relevant information, and stores the results in a local JSON file.

- **Agents Involved:**

- **WeatherFetcherAgent:** Fetches weather data from an external API.
- **DataProcessorAgent:** Processes the fetched data to extract temperature and humidity.
- **DataStorageAgent:** Stores the processed data in a local JSON file.

Step-by-Step Guide:

1. **Initialize the Project:**

bash

```
mkdir api-data-workflow
cd api-data-workflow
npm init -y
npm install langgraph.js axios
```

2. **Create index.js:**

bash

```
touch index.js
```

3. **Obtain an API Key:**

For this project, we'll use the OpenWeatherMap API to fetch weather data. Sign up for a free account to obtain an API key.

4. **Write the Workflow Code:**

Open index.js in your code editor and add the following code:

javascript

```
// Import LangGraph.js, Axios, and File System
const LangGraph = require('langgraph.js');
const axios = require('axios');
```

```javascript
const fs = require('fs').promises;

// Create a new LangGraph instance
const graph = new LangGraph();

// Define WeatherFetcherAgent: Fetches weather data from OpenWeatherMap API
graph.addAgent('WeatherFetcherAgent', async (context) => {
  try {
    const apiKey = 'YOUR_API_KEY'; // Replace with your actual API key
    const city = 'London';
    const url = `https://api.openweathermap.org/data/2.5/weather?q=${city}&appid=${apiKey}&units=metric`;

    const response = await axios.get(url);
    context.data.weather = response.data;
    console.log('WeatherFetcherAgent: Weather data fetched successfully.');
    context.next();
  } catch (error) {
    console.error('WeatherFetcherAgent encountered an error:', error.message);
    context.stop(); // Halts the workflow on error
  }
});

// Define DataProcessorAgent: Processes fetched weather data
graph.addAgent('DataProcessorAgent', async (context) => {
  try {
```

```javascript
    const weatherData = context.data.weather;
    const processedData = {
      city: weatherData.name,
      temperature: weatherData.main.temp,
      humidity: weatherData.main.humidity,
      description: weatherData.weather[0].description,
      timestamp: new Date(),
    };
    context.data.processedWeather = processedData;
    console.log('DataProcessorAgent: Weather data processed successfully.');
    context.next();
  } catch (error) {
    console.error('DataProcessorAgent encountered an error:', error.message);
    context.stop(); // Halts the workflow on error
  }
});

// Define DataStorageAgent: Stores processed data in a local JSON file
graph.addAgent('DataStorageAgent', async (context) => {
  try {
    const processedWeather = context.data.processedWeather;
    const filePath = 'weatherData.json';

    // Read existing data
    let existingData = [];
    try {
      const data = await fs.readFile(filePath, 'utf8');
      existingData = JSON.parse(data);
```

```
    } catch (readError) {
      if (readError.code !== 'ENOENT') {
        throw readError; // Re-throw if it's not a file not found error
      }
      // If file doesn't exist, start with an empty array
    }

    // Append new data
    existingData.push(processedWeather);

    // Write updated data back to the file
    await fs.writeFile(filePath, JSON.stringify(existingData, null, 2));
    console.log('DataStorageAgent: Processed weather data stored successfully.');
    context.next();
  } catch (error) {
    console.error('DataStorageAgent encountered an error:', error.message);
    context.stop(); // Halts the workflow on error
  }
});

// Define the workflow sequence
graph.defineWorkflow('weatherDataWorkflow', [
  'WeatherFetcherAgent',
  'DataProcessorAgent',
  'DataStorageAgent',
]);
```

```javascript
// Run the workflow
graph
  .run('weatherDataWorkflow')
  .then(() => {
    console.log('Weather Data Workflow completed successfully.');
  })
  .catch((error) => {
    console.error('Weather Data Workflow encountered an error:', error);
  });
```

5. **Code Explanation:**
    o **Importing Libraries:**

javascript

```javascript
const LangGraph = require('langgraph.js');
const axios = require('axios');
const fs = require('fs').promises;
```
Imports LangGraph.js for workflow management, Axios for making HTTP requests, and the File System module for file operations.

    o **Creating LangGraph Instance:**

javascript

```javascript
const graph = new LangGraph();
```
Initializes a new LangGraph instance to manage agents and workflows.

    o **Defining WeatherFetcherAgent:**

javascript

```javascript
graph.addAgent('WeatherFetcherAgent', async (context) => {
  try {
    const apiKey = 'YOUR_API_KEY'; // Replace with your actual API key
    const city = 'London';
    const url = `https://api.openweathermap.org/data/2.5/weather?q=${city}&appid=${apiKey}&units=metric`;

    const response = await axios.get(url);
    context.data.weather = response.data;
    console.log('WeatherFetcherAgent: Weather data fetched successfully.');
    context.next();
  } catch (error) {
    console.error('WeatherFetcherAgent encountered an error:', error.message);
    context.stop(); // Halts the workflow on error
  }
});
```

- **Function:** Fetches weather data from the OpenWeatherMap API for the specified city.
- **Data Storage:** Stores the fetched data in context.data.weather.
- **Error Handling:** Catches and logs errors, halting the workflow if an error occurs.

o **Defining DataProcessorAgent:**

javascript

```javascript
graph.addAgent('DataProcessorAgent', async (context) => {
  try {
```

```javascript
    const weatherData = context.data.weather;
    const processedData = {
      city: weatherData.name,
      temperature: weatherData.main.temp,
      humidity: weatherData.main.humidity,
      description: weatherData.weather[0].description,
      timestamp: new Date(),
    };
    context.data.processedWeather = processedData;
    console.log('DataProcessorAgent: Weather data processed successfully.');
    context.next();
  } catch (error) {
    console.error('DataProcessorAgent encountered an error:', error.message);
    context.stop(); // Halts the workflow on error
  }
});
```

- **Function:** Processes the fetched weather data to extract relevant information such as temperature, humidity, and description.
- **Data Storage:** Stores the processed data in context.data.processedWeather.
- **Error Handling:** Catches and logs errors, halting the workflow if an error occurs.

  o **Defining DataStorageAgent:**

javascript

```javascript
graph.addAgent('DataStorageAgent', async (context) => {
  try {
    const processedWeather = context.data.processedWeather;
```

```
    const filePath = 'weatherData.json';

    // Read existing data
    let existingData = [];
    try {
      const data = await fs.readFile(filePath, 'utf8');
      existingData = JSON.parse(data);
    } catch (readError) {
      if (readError.code !== 'ENOENT') {
        throw readError; // Re-throw if it's not a file not found error
      }
      // If file doesn't exist, start with an empty array
    }

    // Append new data
    existingData.push(processedWeather);

    // Write updated data back to the file
    await fs.writeFile(filePath, JSON.stringify(existingData, null, 2));
    console.log('DataStorageAgent: Processed weather data stored successfully.');
    context.next();
  } catch (error) {
    console.error('DataStorageAgent encountered an error:', error.message);
    context.stop(); // Halts the workflow on error
  }
});
```

- **Function:** Stores the processed weather data in a local JSON file named weatherData.json.

- **Data Handling:** Reads existing data, appends new data, and writes back to the file.
- **Error Handling:** Catches and logs errors, halting the workflow if an error occurs.

o **Defining the Workflow:**

javascript

```javascript
graph.defineWorkflow('weatherDataWorkflow', [
  'WeatherFetcherAgent',
  'DataProcessorAgent',
  'DataStorageAgent',
]);
```

- **Workflow Name:** weatherDataWorkflow
- **Sequence:** Defines the order of agent execution.

o **Running the Workflow:**

javascript

```javascript
graph
  .run('weatherDataWorkflow')
  .then(() => {
    console.log('Weather Data Workflow completed successfully.');
  })
  .catch((error) => {
    console.error('Weather Data Workflow encountered an error:', error);
  });
```

- Initiates the workflow and handles success or error outcomes.

- **Helper Functions:**
    - **processData:** Processes the combined data. In this example, it merges the data and adds a timestamp.
    - **storeData:** Stores the processed data. Currently, it logs the data but can be expanded to perform actual storage operations.

6. **Replace the API Key:**

In the WeatherFetcherAgent, replace 'YOUR_API_KEY' with your actual OpenWeatherMap API key.

javascript

```
const apiKey = 'YOUR_ACTUAL_API_KEY';
```

7. **Execute the Workflow:**

Run the workflow using the following command in your terminal:

bash

```
node index.js
```

8. **Expected Output:**

kotlin

WeatherFetcherAgent: Weather data fetched successfully.

DataProcessorAgent: Weather data processed successfully.

DataStorageAgent: Processed weather data stored successfully.

Weather Data Workflow completed successfully.

Additionally, a weatherData.json file will be created (if it doesn't already exist) and updated with the processed weather data:

json

```
[
  {
    "city": "London",
    "temperature": 15,
    "humidity": 82,
    "description": "light rain",
    "timestamp": "2024-12-18T12:34:56.789Z"
  }
]
```

Project Insights:

- **Agent Collaboration:** Each agent handles a distinct part of the workflow, ensuring separation of concerns and modularity.

- **Asynchronous Operations:** The use of async/await in agents allows for non-blocking execution, enabling concurrent tasks.

- **Error Handling:** Robust error handling within each agent ensures that failures are managed gracefully, preventing the entire workflow from crashing.

- **Data Flow Management:** The context object facilitates the flow of data between agents, maintaining a clear and organized data structure.

- **Scalability:** This workflow can be easily extended by adding more agents or integrating additional data sources without significant restructuring.

Best Practices Demonstrated:

- **Modular Design:** Each agent has a single responsibility, promoting reusability and ease of maintenance.

- **Asynchronous Programming:** Leveraging JavaScript's asynchronous capabilities ensures efficient task execution.

- **Robust Error Handling:** Implementing try-catch blocks within agents prevents unhandled exceptions and workflow disruptions.

- **Clear Data Management:** Using the context object to store and pass data ensures that agents have access to the necessary information without tight coupling.

Summary

In **Chapter 2**, we've explored the core concepts that form the backbone of LangGraph.js workflows. You learned about agents and their roles within workflows, the structure of nodes and graphs, and the significance of asynchronous processing in managing concurrency. Through practical examples and a hands-on mini-project, you gained valuable insights into designing and implementing effective workflows using LangGraph.js.

Key Takeaways:

- **Agents:** Autonomous entities that perform specific tasks within a workflow.

- **Workflows:** Structured sequences of agent executions designed to achieve particular objectives.

- **Nodes and Graphs:** The structural components that define the relationships and data flow between agents.

- **Asynchronous Processing:** Essential for managing concurrent tasks, ensuring efficient and non-blocking execution.

Chapter 3: Building Intelligent Agents

In this chapter, we explore how to build intelligent agents by understanding their architecture, communication mechanisms, and how to handle errors efficiently in complex workflows. By the end of this chapter, you'll have a deep understanding of agent behavior, message passing, real-time communication, and resilient error handling strategies.

3.1 Agent Architectures

In LangGraph.js, agents are at the heart of the workflow, performing specific tasks autonomously. The architecture of an agent defines how it interacts with other agents and the environment. There are different types of agent architectures, which influence how agents behave and how they are integrated into workflows. In this section, we'll examine reactive vs. proactive agents and stateless vs. stateful agents.

3.1.1 Reactive vs. Proactive Agents

Understanding the difference between reactive and proactive agents is key to designing workflows that fit specific tasks and goals. These two types of agents have different behaviors and interaction models.

Reactive Agents:

- **Definition:** Reactive agents respond to stimuli or events from the environment. They act based on predefined rules, and they do not plan ahead or maintain any internal state beyond their current task.

- **Characteristics:**
    - **Event-Driven:** Reactive agents are triggered by events or conditions.
    - **No Planning:** They do not anticipate future tasks but instead respond as needed.

- **Simplicity:** These agents typically have simpler implementations, as they only react to external stimuli.
- **Example:** Imagine a chatbot agent that only responds when a user asks a specific question. If the user asks, "What time is it?", the agent will reply with the current time. However, it won't initiate any further actions unless prompted by the user.

Proactive Agents:

- **Definition:** Proactive agents, on the other hand, take the initiative and anticipate future events. They are goal-oriented and can plan, act, and adapt their behavior based on a series of objectives or events.
- **Characteristics:**
    - **Goal-Oriented:** Proactive agents work toward achieving specific objectives.
    - **Planning:** They can predict future events and plan their actions accordingly.
    - **Adaptability:** They can adapt to changes in the environment based on their goals and plans.
    - **Stateful:** They typically retain memory of past events, allowing them to make decisions based on previous experiences.
- **Example:** A proactive agent could be a recommendation system in an e-commerce platform. It might track a user's browsing history and purchase behavior to anticipate future needs and proactively suggest products, even without the user explicitly asking for recommendations.

Comparison Table: Reactive vs. Proactive Agents

Aspect	Reactive Agents	Proactive Agents
Behavior	Reacts to events and stimuli	Initiates actions based on goals or predictions

Aspect	Reactive Agents	Proactive Agents
State	Stateless, does not maintain memory	Stateful, retains information for future actions
Flexibility	Limited, responds only to current conditions	More flexible, adapts based on context and goals
Complexity	Simpler, easier to implement	More complex, requires planning and adaptation
Use Cases	Event-driven systems like alert systems, notifications	Systems requiring goal-oriented behavior, such as recommendation engines, planning systems
Advantages	Simple, efficient	Can anticipate and adapt to changes, making them more robust
Limitations	Limited interaction, lacks anticipation	More computationally intensive, requires more resources

3.1.2 Stateless vs. Stateful Agents

Agents in LangGraph.js can be either stateless or stateful. This distinction determines whether an agent retains information about previous interactions and how it handles context during workflow execution.

Stateless Agents:

- **Definition:** Stateless agents do not maintain any memory of previous interactions. They process each event or task independently, and they do not retain information from one task to the next.
- **Characteristics:**

- - **No History:** Every interaction is treated as a separate event.
  - **Simplicity:** Stateless agents are simpler to implement since they do not require mechanisms for managing state.
  - **Efficiency:** These agents consume fewer resources as they do not store any historical data.
- **Example:** A stateless agent could be a data-fetching agent that simply retrieves data from an API. Once the data is retrieved, the agent does not store the data or use it in any future operations.

Stateful Agents:

- **Definition:** Stateful agents retain information about past interactions, allowing them to maintain a context that can influence future actions.
- **Characteristics:**
  - **Memory:** Stateful agents store information about previous events or tasks, which can affect their decisions or actions in the future.
  - **Complexity:** They are more complex to design and manage, as they require mechanisms for storing and updating state.
  - **Adaptability:** State allows these agents to make informed decisions based on their previous experiences or the context they have accumulated.
- **Example:** A stateful agent might be a user session manager in a web application. It keeps track of a user's actions and preferences throughout their session, enabling personalized responses or actions based on previous activity.

Comparison Table: Stateless vs. Stateful Agents

Aspect	Stateless Agents	Stateful Agents
State Management	Does not store any information	Retains information from previous tasks
Flexibility	Limited flexibility, no context or history	More flexible, adapts based on stored data and context
Complexity	Simple, easy to implement	More complex, requires state management mechanisms
Performance	More efficient, less resource-intensive	More resource-intensive due to state management
Use Cases	Simple tasks, independent actions	Tasks that require context, such as user sessions, complex decision-making
Advantages	Simpler, scalable	More adaptive, capable of more sophisticated behavior
Limitations	Cannot perform tasks that require context	Requires more resources and careful state management

3.2 Agent Communication and Messaging

Effective communication between agents is crucial for building multi-agent systems that work together seamlessly. In this section, we'll look at two primary communication methods: **message passing** and **real-time communication using WebSockets**.

3.2.1 Using Message Passing

Message passing is the most common form of communication between agents. It allows agents to share data, send notifications, or trigger actions in other agents. In LangGraph.js, message passing can be achieved through the context.sendMessage() and context.onMessage() methods.

Key Concepts:

1. **Messages:** A message is a data object that is sent from one agent to another. It can contain any type of information, such as a string, number, object, or even a function.
2. **Send and Receive:** The sendMessage() method is used to send a message, and onMessage() is used to listen for incoming messages.

Example: Simple Message Passing

javascript

```
graph.addAgent('SenderAgent', async (context) => {
  const message = { text: 'Hello, Receiver!' };
  context.sendMessage('ReceiverAgent', message);
  console.log('SenderAgent: Message sent.');
  context.next();
});

graph.addAgent('ReceiverAgent', async (context) => {
  context.onMessage((message) => {
    console.log('ReceiverAgent received:', message.text);
  });
  context.next();
});

graph.defineWorkflow('messageWorkflow', ['SenderAgent', 'ReceiverAgent']);
graph.run('messageWorkflow');
```

Explanation:

- **SenderAgent:** Creates a message object and sends it to ReceiverAgent using context.sendMessage.
- **ReceiverAgent:** Listens for incoming messages using context.onMessage and logs the message when it is received.

Expected Output:

yaml

SenderAgent: Message sent.

ReceiverAgent received: Hello, Receiver!

Best Practices for Message Passing:
- **Consistent Message Structure:** Define a clear structure for messages to avoid confusion and ensure smooth data transfer between agents.
- **Asynchronous Communication:** Use asynchronous messaging to allow agents to continue executing without waiting for a response, reducing bottlenecks.
- **Error Handling:** Implement proper error handling for cases where messages are not delivered or processed correctly.

3.2.2 WebSocket Integration for Real-Time Communication

WebSockets enable real-time, two-way communication between clients and servers, making them ideal for applications requiring instant data transmission, such as live notifications or chat systems.

LangGraph.js can be integrated with WebSockets to allow agents to communicate in real-time. Here, we'll demonstrate how to use **Socket.io**, a popular WebSocket library for Node.js, to enable real-time communication between agents.

Step-by-Step Implementation:
1. **Install Dependencies:**

bash

```
npm install socket.io
```

2. **Setup WebSocket Server:**

javascript

```javascript
const LangGraph = require('langgraph.js');
const http = require('http');
const socketIo = require('socket.io');

const server = http.createServer();
const io = socketIo(server);

const graph = new LangGraph();

// WebSocket listener agent
graph.addAgent('WebSocketListener', async (context) => {
  io.on('connection', (socket) => {
    console.log('New client connected.');

    socket.on('sendMessage', (message) => {
      console.log('WebSocketListener received message:', message);
      io.emit('broadcastMessage', message);
    });

    socket.on('disconnect', () => {
      console.log('Client disconnected.');
    });
  });
});
```

```
    context.next();
  });

  // Start the server and run the workflow
  server.listen(3000, () => {
    console.log('WebSocket server running on port 3000');
  });
  graph.defineWorkflow('webSocketWorkflow',
  ['WebSocketListener']);
  graph.run('webSocketWorkflow');
```

Code Explanation:

- **Socket.io Server:** Creates an HTTP server and initializes Socket.io to listen for WebSocket connections.

- **WebSocketListener Agent:** This agent listens for incoming WebSocket connections. It listens for messages and broadcasts them to all connected clients.

- **Running the Workflow:** The WebSocketListener agent is added to the workflow, and the server listens for WebSocket connections on port 3000.

Client Example:

To test the WebSocket communication, you can create a simple client using HTML and JavaScript to send and receive messages via WebSocket.

html

```html
<!DOCTYPE html>
<html lang="en">
<head>
  <meta charset="UTF-8">
  <meta name="viewport" content="width=device-width, initial-scale=1.0">
```

```html
    <title>WebSocket Test</title>
  </head>
  <body>
    <h1>WebSocket Test</h1>
    <input type="text" id="messageInput">
    <button id="sendButton">Send Message</button>
    <ul id="messagesList"></ul>

    <script src="https://cdn.socket.io/4.4.1/socket.io.min.js"></script>
    <script>
      const socket = io('http://localhost:3000');
      const sendButton = document.getElementById('sendButton');
      const messageInput = document.getElementById('messageInput');
      const messagesList = document.getElementById('messagesList');

      sendButton.addEventListener('click', () => {
        const message = messageInput.value;
        socket.emit('sendMessage', message);
      });

      socket.on('broadcastMessage', (message) => {
        const li = document.createElement('li');
        li.textContent = `Received: ${message}`;
        messagesList.appendChild(li);
      });
    </script>
  </body>
</html>
```

Expected Output:

- Open the HTML file in multiple browser windows.
- When a message is sent in one window, it should be broadcasted to all open clients in real time.

3.3 Error Handling in Workflows

Error handling is crucial in building resilient agent workflows. In this section, we'll cover strategies for graceful failures, retry mechanisms, and circuit breakers to manage errors effectively.

3.3.1 Graceful Failures

Graceful failure refers to handling errors in a way that prevents the entire system from crashing and ensures that users are informed appropriately.

- **Try-Catch Blocks:** Use try-catch blocks in asynchronous code to catch and handle errors gracefully.
- **Context Stop:** If an error occurs that should halt the workflow, use context.stop() to stop further agent execution.
- **Logging:** Always log the error messages to keep track of issues and for debugging purposes.

Example: Graceful Failure in an Agent

javascript

```javascript
graph.addAgent('RiskyAgent', async (context) => {
  try {
    const result = await performRiskyOperation();
    context.data.result = result;
    context.next();
  } catch (error) {
    console.error('RiskyAgent encountered an error:', error.message);
```

```
    context.stop(); // Halts the workflow if an error occurs
  }
});
```

Code Explanation:

- The RiskyAgent attempts to perform a risky operation.
- If the operation fails, the error is caught, logged, and the workflow is halted using context.stop().

3.3.2 Retry Strategies and Circuit Breakers

To enhance the resilience of workflows, implement **retry strategies** and **circuit breakers**. These mechanisms prevent the workflow from failing completely when temporary errors occur.

- **Retry Strategies:** Retry failed operations a fixed number of times with exponential backoff to reduce the strain on the system.
- **Circuit Breakers:** Prevent repeated failures by opening the circuit after a threshold of errors is reached, stopping further attempts until the system recovers.

Example: Retry Strategy with Exponential Backoff

javascript

```javascript
graph.addAgent('RetryAgent', async (context) => {
  let attempt = 0;
  const maxRetries = 3;

  const fetchDataWithRetry = async () => {
    try {
      const data = await fetchData();
      context.data.fetchedData = data;
      context.next();
    } catch (error) {
```

```
    if (attempt < maxRetries) {
      attempt++;
      const delayTime = Math.pow(2, attempt) * 1000; // Exponential backoff
      console.log(`RetryAgent: Attempt ${attempt} failed. Retrying in ${delayTime / 1000} seconds.`);
      await new Promise((resolve) => setTimeout(resolve, delayTime));
      fetchDataWithRetry(); // Retry the operation
    } else {
      console.error('RetryAgent: Max retries reached. Stopping workflow.');
      context.stop(); // Halts the workflow after max retries
    }
   }
  };

  fetchDataWithRetry();
});
```

Code Explanation:

- **Retry Logic:** The agent attempts to fetch data. If it fails, it waits for an exponentially increasing period before retrying.
- **Max Retry Limit:** The agent stops after 3 failed attempts.

3.3.3 Exercise: Handling Failures Gracefully in a Chatbot Workflow

To demonstrate error handling, let's build a simple chatbot workflow. The chatbot will receive user input, process it, and respond. We'll add error handling to ensure the chatbot gracefully handles invalid input or failures.

Workflow Overview:

1. **UserInputAgent:** Receives user input and processes it.
2. **ResponseAgent:** Generates a response based on input.
3. **LoggingAgent:** Logs the interaction for later analysis.

Step-by-Step Instructions:

1. **Initialize the Project:**

bash

```
mkdir chatbot-error-handling
cd chatbot-error-handling
npm init -y
npm install langgraph.js
```

2. **Create index.js:**

bash

```
touch index.js
```

3. **Write the Workflow Code:**

javascript

```
const LangGraph = require('langgraph.js');

const graph = new LangGraph();

graph.addAgent('UserInputAgent', async (context) => {
  try {
    const userInput = context.data.input;
```

```javascript
    if (!userInput) {
      throw new Error('User input is missing.');
    }
    context.data.processedInput = userInput.trim().toLowerCase();
    context.next();
  } catch (error) {
    console.error('UserInputAgent Error:', error.message);
    context.stop(); // Halts the workflow if input is invalid
  }
});

graph.addAgent('ResponseAgent', async (context) => {
  try {
    const input = context.data.processedInput;
    let response;

    switch (input) {
      case 'hello':
        response = 'Hello! How can I help you?';
        break;
      case 'help':
        response = 'I can assist with FAQs.';
        break;
      default:
        response = 'Sorry, I did not understand that.';
    }

    context.data.response = response;
    context.next();
  } catch (error) {
```

```javascript
    console.error('ResponseAgent Error:', error.message);
    context.stop();
  }
});

graph.addAgent('LoggingAgent', async (context) => {
  try {
    const input = context.data.processedInput;
    const response = context.data.response;
    console.log(`User: ${input}, Bot: ${response}`);
    context.next();
  } catch (error) {
    console.error('LoggingAgent Error:', error.message);
    context.stop();
  }
});

graph.defineWorkflow('chatbotWorkflow', ['UserInputAgent', 'ResponseAgent', 'LoggingAgent']);

const runChatbot = async (input) => {
  try {
    graph.run('chatbotWorkflow', { input })
      .then(() => {
        console.log('Chatbot Workflow completed successfully.');
      })
      .catch((error) => {
        console.error('Chatbot Workflow encountered an error:', error);
      });
```

```
  } catch (error) {
    console.error('Error during user input simulation:',
error.message);
  }
};

// Simulate successful user interaction
runChatbot('hello');
runChatbot('help');

// Simulate an error
runChatbot('');
```

Code Explanation:

- **UserInputAgent:** Receives user input and processes it. If no input is provided, it throws an error.
- **ResponseAgent:** Generates a response based on user input.
- **LoggingAgent:** Logs the user input and bot response.
- **Error Handling:** If any agent encounters an error, it logs the error and halts the workflow.

Expected Output:

python

```
User: hello, Bot: Hello! How can I help you?
Chatbot Workflow completed successfully.

User: help, Bot: I can assist with FAQs.
Chatbot Workflow completed successfully.
```

```
UserInputAgent Error: User input is missing.
```

Summary

In **Chapter 3**, we covered the foundations of building intelligent agents in LangGraph.js. We discussed the differences between reactive and proactive agents, as well as stateless and stateful agents. We also explored communication strategies like message passing and WebSocket integration for real-time interactions between agents. Additionally, we learned essential error handling techniques, such as graceful failure, retry strategies, and circuit breakers, to ensure your workflows are robust and resilient.

Key Takeaways:

- **Agent Architectures:** Understand the difference between reactive and proactive agents, as well as stateless and stateful agents, to design effective workflows.

- **Agent Communication:** Use message passing and WebSocket integration to enable seamless communication between agents.

- **Error Handling:** Implement strategies for graceful failure, retries, and circuit breakers to make your workflows more resilient and fault-tolerant.

- **Practical Application:** Through exercises, you learned how to implement these strategies in a real-world chatbot workflow.

Chapter 4: Scaling Multi-Agent Systems

In this chapter, we will explore strategies for scaling multi-agent systems to meet performance demands. LangGraph.js offers the flexibility to build large, complex workflows. As your workflows grow, so do the challenges related to performance, orchestration, and testing. We will look at how to scale workflows efficiently, orchestrate multiple agents, and ensure robust debugging and testing practices.

4.1 Scaling Workflows for Performance

When building multi-agent systems, performance can become a bottleneck if workflows are not optimized. Effective scaling techniques allow systems to handle more agents and tasks without sacrificing speed or reliability. This section will cover managing dependencies between agents and ensuring scalability.

4.1.1 Managing Dependencies Between Agents

In a multi-agent system, agents can have dependencies on each other. For example, one agent may need to receive data from another agent before proceeding with its task. Managing these dependencies is crucial for maintaining performance as the system scales.

Key Concepts:

- **Sequential Dependencies:** Some agents may need to execute in a specific order, with each agent waiting for data from its predecessor.

- **Parallel Execution:** When agents can work independently of each other, they should be executed in parallel to maximize throughput.

- **Dependency Management:** Ensuring that agents only wait for data from dependencies that are required for their execution. This reduces unnecessary delays.

Example: Sequential vs. Parallel Execution

Let's say we have two agents that perform tasks in sequence (one depends on the output of the other). In another case, we have independent tasks that can be executed in parallel.

Sequential Execution:

javascript

```javascript
graph.addAgent('AgentA', async (context) => {
  const data = await fetchDataFromService();
  context.data.serviceData = data;
  context.next();
});

graph.addAgent('AgentB', async (context) => {
  const serviceData = context.data.serviceData;
  const result = await processData(serviceData);
  context.data.result = result;
  context.next();
});

graph.defineWorkflow('sequentialWorkflow', ['AgentA', 'AgentB']);
graph.run('sequentialWorkflow');
```

- **Explanation:**
    - **AgentA** fetches data from a service and passes it to **AgentB**.
    - **AgentB** uses the data from **AgentA** to perform further processing.
    - The agents execute in a sequence, ensuring that **AgentB** runs only after **AgentA** has completed.

Parallel Execution:

javascript

```javascript
graph.addAgent('AgentA', async (context) => {
  const dataA = await fetchDataFromServiceA();
  context.data.dataA = dataA;
  context.next();
});

graph.addAgent('AgentB', async (context) => {
  const dataB = await fetchDataFromServiceB();
  context.data.dataB = dataB;
  context.next();
});

graph.addAgent('AgentC', async (context) => {
  const dataA = context.data.dataA;
  const dataB = context.data.dataB;
  const result = await processBothData(dataA, dataB);
  context.data.result = result;
  context.next();
});

graph.defineWorkflow('parallelWorkflow', ['AgentA', 'AgentB', 'AgentC']);
graph.run('parallelWorkflow');
```

- **Explanation:**
    o **AgentA** and **AgentB** execute in parallel, independently fetching data from different services.

- **AgentC** processes the data from both agents once both **AgentA** and **AgentB** have completed.

Best Practices:

- **Minimize Sequential Dependencies:** Design your workflows so that as many agents as possible can run in parallel to improve performance.

- **Efficient Data Sharing:** Use shared contexts and data objects to pass information between agents to avoid redundant computations.

- **Optimize Data Fetching:** Use batching or parallel requests for external API calls to reduce latency.

4.1.2 Ensuring Scalability and Performance

As the number of agents and tasks increases, it's crucial to ensure that the system can handle larger workloads without becoming sluggish or unresponsive. Below are a few strategies for ensuring scalability:

1. Load Balancing:

- **Distribute Workload:** Distribute agent tasks across multiple servers or processes to balance the load. This prevents a single server from becoming a bottleneck.

- **Horizontal Scaling:** Add more servers or instances to handle increased load rather than upgrading a single server (vertical scaling).

2. Caching and Data Optimization:

- **Cache Results:** Store frequently accessed data or computation results in a cache to avoid redundant operations.

- **Efficient Data Structures:** Use efficient data structures for storing and accessing agent data, such as hash maps or priority queues.

3. Asynchronous Execution:

- **Async Operations:** Use asynchronous operations to ensure that agents don't block the execution of other agents when waiting for external resources.

- **Event-Driven Execution:** Implement event-driven systems where agents listen for events rather than continuously polling for data.

Example: Scaling an API Workflow Using Caching

javascript

```javascript
graph.addAgent('APICacheAgent', async (context) => {
  const cacheKey = 'apiData';
  let data = await getCache(cacheKey);

  if (!data) {
    data = await fetchDataFromAPI();
    await setCache(cacheKey, data); // Store data in cache for future use
  }

  context.data.apiData = data;
  context.next();
});
```

- **Explanation:** This agent first checks the cache before making an API call, improving performance by reducing redundant data fetching.

4.2 Workflow Orchestration

Orchestrating multiple agents is an essential skill for managing complex workflows. This section will focus on two primary concepts: using coordinators and handling workflow failures.

4.2.1 Using Coordinators

Coordinators are agents that manage the execution of multiple agents, deciding when they should run and in what order. They can also handle dependencies between agents and orchestrate their execution for maximum efficiency.

Key Concepts:

- **Centralized vs. Decentralized Coordination:** In a centralized system, one agent (the coordinator) decides the execution order, while in decentralized systems, agents can autonomously decide when to execute based on their state or input.
- **Coordinated Execution:** Coordinators can ensure that agents that depend on each other run in the right order.

Example: Using a Coordinator to Manage Multiple Agents

javascript

```
graph.addAgent('Coordinator', async (context) => {
  console.log('Starting the workflow...');

  // Coordinating the execution of dependent agents
  await context.run('AgentA');
  await context.run('AgentB');

  console.log('All agents executed successfully.');
  context.next();
});

graph.addAgent('AgentA', async (context) => {
  // Do something
  console.log('AgentA executed.');
  context.next();
});

graph.addAgent('AgentB', async (context) => {
```

```
  // Do something else
  console.log('AgentB executed.');
  context.next();
});

graph.defineWorkflow('coordinatedWorkflow', ['Coordinator', 'AgentA', 'AgentB']);
graph.run('coordinatedWorkflow');
```

- **Explanation:** The Coordinator agent manages the execution of **AgentA** and **AgentB**, ensuring they execute in sequence. The use of context.run() allows for explicit control over agent execution.

Best Practices for Orchestration:

- **Centralized Coordination:** Use a centralized coordinator to ensure that workflows are executed in the correct order.
- **Dynamic Workflow Adjustments:** Allow the coordinator to adjust the execution flow based on real-time data or conditions.

4.2.2 Handling Workflow Failures and Recovery

Workflow failures are inevitable in complex systems. It's essential to build recovery strategies that can either continue the workflow or alert the system administrators when something goes wrong.

Key Concepts:

- **Error Handling:** Implement try-catch blocks in agents to catch and manage errors.
- **Graceful Recovery:** Provide mechanisms that allow workflows to continue even after an error, if possible.
- **Rollback Strategies:** In case of a critical failure, implement a rollback strategy to revert to a safe state.

Example: Workflow Recovery with Fallback Agents

javascript

```javascript
graph.addAgent('RiskyAgent', async (context) => {
  try {
    const data = await fetchDataFromRiskyService();
    context.data.result = data;
    context.next();
  } catch (error) {
    console.error('Error in RiskyAgent:', error.message);
    // Fallback action: Execute the SafeAgent
    await context.run('SafeAgent');
  }
});

graph.addAgent('SafeAgent', async (context) => {
  console.log('Executing SafeAgent due to failure in RiskyAgent.');
  context.data.result = 'Safe result';
  context.next();
});

graph.defineWorkflow('failureRecoveryWorkflow', ['RiskyAgent']);
graph.run('failureRecoveryWorkflow');
```

- **Explanation:** If **RiskyAgent** fails, the SafeAgent will execute as a fallback to ensure that the workflow continues.

4.3 Debugging and Testing Multi-Agent Systems

As your workflows become more complex, debugging and testing become essential to ensure that everything works as expected. In this section, we will focus on unit testing workflows, advanced testing techniques, and stress testing multi-agent systems.

4.3.1 Unit Testing for Workflows

Unit testing is the practice of testing individual components (agents) of the workflow to ensure they behave as expected. LangGraph.js workflows can be tested using testing frameworks such as **Jest** or **Mocha**.

Key Concepts:

- **Mocking Dependencies:** Use mocks to simulate external services or agents that a workflow depends on.
- **Isolated Testing:** Test each agent in isolation before integrating them into a larger workflow.

Example: Unit Test for an Agent

javascript

```javascript
const { runWorkflow } = require('langgraph.js'); // Mocked LangGraph.js import
const { expect } = require('chai');

describe('RiskyAgent', () => {
  it('should fetch data correctly', async () => {
    const result = await runWorkflow('RiskyAgent', { input: 'test' });
    expect(result).to.equal('expected output');
  });
});
```

- **Explanation:** This test ensures that **RiskyAgent** behaves as expected when provided with specific input.

4.3.2 Advanced Testing Techniques

Advanced testing techniques involve testing the system as a whole, ensuring that agents work together correctly in complex workflows.

Key Concepts:

- **Integration Testing:** Test the entire workflow to ensure all agents work together as expected.
- **End-to-End Testing:** Test workflows in real-world conditions, simulating user interactions.

4.3.3 Example: Stress Testing a Workflow with 10,000 Concurrent Agents

Stress testing helps identify performance issues by simulating high levels of activity, such as running 10,000 concurrent agents.

Example: Stress Testing with Concurrent Agents

javascript

```javascript
const { graph } = require('langgraph.js'); // Mocked LangGraph.js import

const stressTest = async () => {
  const agents = Array(10000).fill('TestAgent');
  graph.addAgent('TestAgent', async (context) => {
    context.data.result = 'processed';
    context.next();
  });

  graph.defineWorkflow('stressTestWorkflow', agents);
  await graph.run('stressTestWorkflow');
};

stressTest();
```

- **Explanation:** This code simulates the execution of 10,000 concurrent agents to test the system's performance under heavy load.

Chapter Summary

In **Chapter 4**, we learned how to scale multi-agent systems for performance, effectively orchestrate workflows, and handle failures. We also explored strategies for debugging and testing multi-agent workflows to ensure that they perform well under different conditions.

Key Takeaways:

- **Scaling Performance:** Efficiently manage dependencies between agents, parallelize tasks where possible, and optimize data handling.

- **Orchestrating Workflows:** Use coordinators to manage agent execution and implement recovery strategies to handle errors gracefully.

- **Debugging and Testing:** Unit tests, integration tests, and stress tests are essential for ensuring the robustness and scalability of your workflows.

Chapter 5: Integrating LangGraph.js with Web Applications

LangGraph.js is a powerful tool for building complex agent-based workflows, but its true potential shines when integrated into web applications. This chapter will guide you through the process of integrating LangGraph.js workflows into both the **frontend** and **backend** of a web application. We will explore how to connect LangGraph.js with React.js for dynamic, interactive user interfaces, how to build dashboards to monitor agents in real-time, and how to connect your workflows with backend frameworks like Express.js. We will also dive into building real-time applications, including chatbots, streaming data processors, and a live notification system.

5.1 Frontend Integrations

Frontend integration allows LangGraph.js workflows to be triggered and monitored directly from the user interface. By combining LangGraph.js with popular frontend frameworks like **React.js**, you can create highly interactive and real-time web applications.

5.1.1 Connecting LangGraph.js Workflows with React.js

React.js is a widely-used library for building dynamic user interfaces. Integrating LangGraph.js workflows with React allows you to trigger, interact with, and display results from workflows directly in the UI.

Key Concepts:

- **State Management:** React's component state can be used to store and update the results of LangGraph.js workflows.

- **Event Handling:** User interactions such as button clicks or form submissions can trigger workflows.

Example: Triggering a LangGraph.js Workflow in React

1. **Install Dependencies:** Make sure you have langgraph.js and react set up. If not, you can install langgraph.js via npm:

bash

```
npm install langgraph.js
```

2. **Creating a React Component to Trigger LangGraph.js Workflow:**

javascript

```
import React, { useState } from 'react';
import LangGraph from 'langgraph.js';

// Create LangGraph instance
const graph = new LangGraph();

// Define a simple agent workflow
graph.addAgent('AgentA', async (context) => {
  const result = await fetchDataFromAPI();
  context.data.apiResult = result;
  context.next();
});

graph.defineWorkflow('simpleWorkflow', ['AgentA']);

const App = () => {
  const [workflowResult, setWorkflowResult] = useState(null);

  // Function to trigger the workflow
  const runWorkflow = async () => {
    try {
      await graph.run('simpleWorkflow');
```

```
      setWorkflowResult(graph.getData().apiResult); //
Display result in the UI
    } catch (error) {
      console.error('Workflow failed:', error);
    }
  };

  return (
    <div>
      <h1>LangGraph.js Workflow with React</h1>
      <button onClick={runWorkflow}>Run Workflow</button>
      {workflowResult && <p>API Result: {workflowResult}</p>}
    </div>
  );
};

export default App;
```

Explanation:

- **Graph Setup:** A LangGraph.js instance is created, and a simple agent (AgentA) is added that fetches data from an API (simulated in the example).

- **Triggering the Workflow:** The runWorkflow function is triggered when the button is clicked. It starts the LangGraph.js workflow and updates the UI with the results using React's state management (setWorkflowResult).

- **Displaying Results:** Once the workflow completes, the result is displayed on the page.

Best Practices for Integrating LangGraph.js with React:

- **Use State Hooks:** React's useState and useEffect hooks are ideal for handling workflow results and re-rendering the UI.

- **Error Handling:** Always implement error handling to ensure that the UI remains responsive, even if something goes wrong with the workflow.

- **Async Operations:** LangGraph.js workflows are asynchronous, so React's asynchronous handling (like async/await) should be used when triggering and waiting for workflows.

5.1.2 Building Interactive Dashboards for Monitoring Agents

Real-time monitoring of agent workflows can provide valuable insights into the state of your system. Dashboards allow you to track the status of agents, view logs, and monitor performance. This is especially important when working with complex multi-agent systems.

Key Concepts:

- **Live Data Updates:** React can be used to update the UI dynamically as the agent workflow progresses.
- **Charts and Graphs:** Use charting libraries like **Chart.js** or **Recharts** to visualize data dynamically.

Example: Simple Dashboard to Monitor Agent Status

1. **Install Chart.js and React-Chartjs-2 for Visualization:**

bash

```
npm install chart.js react-chartjs-2
```

2. **Dashboard Component to Display Agent Progress:**

javascript

```javascript
import React, { useState } from 'react';
import { Line } from 'react-chartjs-2';
import LangGraph from 'langgraph.js';
import { Chart as ChartJS, CategoryScale, LinearScale, PointElement, LineElement } from 'chart.js';

ChartJS.register(CategoryScale, LinearScale, PointElement, LineElement);

// Initialize LangGraph.js
const graph = new LangGraph();

// Define a simple agent that logs progress
graph.addAgent('AgentA', async (context) => {
  let progress = 0;
  for (let i = 0; i < 10; i++) {
    await new Promise(resolve => setTimeout(resolve, 500)); // Simulate delay
    progress += 10;
    context.data.progress = progress;
    context.next();
  }
});

graph.defineWorkflow('progressWorkflow', ['AgentA']);

const Dashboard = () => {
  const [progressData, setProgressData] = useState([]);

  // Start workflow and collect data for the chart
  const startWorkflow = async () => {
```

```
    await graph.run('progressWorkflow');
    const progress = graph.getData().progress;
    setProgressData(prev => [...prev, progress]);
  };

  // Chart data and options
  const chartData = {
    labels: progressData.map((_, index) => `Step ${index + 1}`),
    datasets: [{
      label: 'Agent Progress',
      data: progressData,
      fill: false,
      borderColor: 'rgba(75, 192, 192, 1)',
      tension: 0.1
    }]
  };

  return (
    <div>
      <h1>Agent Workflow Progress</h1>
      <button onClick={startWorkflow}>Start Workflow</button>
      <Line data={chartData} />
    </div>
  );
};

export default Dashboard;
```
Explanation:

- **Agent Progress Tracking:** The AgentA agent simulates progress through a loop, updating the progress every 500 milliseconds.

- **Dynamic Chart Updates:** The progress is recorded in the progressData state, and the Line chart updates dynamically as the workflow progresses.

- **Chart.js Integration:** The data is fed into a Line chart to visually represent the agent's progress over time.

Best Practices for Building Dashboards:

- **Real-Time Updates:** Use useState and useEffect hooks to update the dashboard in real-time as data changes.

- **Charts and Graphs:** Use charting libraries like **Chart.js** to represent data visually and help users better understand the workflow status.

5.2 Backend Integrations

Backend integration allows LangGraph.js workflows to be triggered and controlled via APIs. This is useful when integrating workflows with server-side applications, databases, and external services.

5.2.1 Using LangGraph.js with Express.js

Express.js is a popular framework for building backend APIs in Node.js. By integrating LangGraph.js with Express, you can trigger workflows based on HTTP requests, interact with databases, and expose the results via REST or GraphQL APIs.

Key Concepts:

- **API Endpoints:** Use Express.js to expose endpoints that trigger LangGraph.js workflows.

- **Async Operations:** Since LangGraph.js workflows are asynchronous, you will need to handle these operations using async/await.

Example: Triggering a LangGraph.js Workflow via Express.js API

1. **Install Express:**

bash

```
npm install express langgraph.js
```

2. **Create Express Server with LangGraph.js Workflow:**

javascript

```javascript
const express = require('express');
const LangGraph = require('langgraph.js');
const app = express();
const port = 3000;

// Initialize LangGraph.js
const graph = new LangGraph();

// Define a simple agent workflow
graph.addAgent('AgentA', async (context) => {
  const data = await fetchDataFromAPI();
  context.data.apiResult = data;
  context.next();
});

graph.defineWorkflow('simpleWorkflow', ['AgentA']);

// Define an Express route to trigger the workflow
app.get('/run-workflow', async (req, res) => {
  try {
    await graph.run('simpleWorkflow');
    res.json({ success: true, data: graph.getData().apiResult });
```

```
  } catch (error) {
    res.status(500).json({ success: false, message: 'Workflow failed', error: error.message });
  }
});

app.listen(port, () => {
  console.log(`Server running at http://localhost:${port}`);
});
```

Explanation:

- **Express Setup:** A basic Express server is created to listen on port 3000.

- **LangGraph.js Workflow:** The server defines a simple LangGraph.js workflow with one agent (AgentA) that fetches data from an API.

- **API Endpoint:** A route (/run-workflow) is exposed to trigger the LangGraph.js workflow. The results of the workflow are returned as a JSON response.

Best Practices for Backend Integrations:

- **Handle Asynchronous Operations:** Use async/await to manage asynchronous workflows.

- **Error Handling:** Ensure that proper error handling is in place, especially when workflows fail or return unexpected results.

- **Security:** Consider adding authentication and authorization mechanisms (e.g., JWT) to protect sensitive workflows and data.

5.2.2 REST and GraphQL APIs for Agent Workflows

Exposing LangGraph.js workflows via **REST** and **GraphQL** APIs allows you to interact with workflows programmatically from external applications. REST APIs are the most common approach, but

GraphQL provides a more flexible way to query and interact with data.

REST APIs:
- Use RESTful endpoints to trigger workflows and return data as JSON.

GraphQL APIs:
- GraphQL allows more complex queries and mutations, enabling clients to request exactly the data they need.

Example: Exposing LangGraph.js Workflow via GraphQL:

1. **Install GraphQL and Apollo Server:**

bash

```
npm install graphql apollo-server-express
```

2. **Create GraphQL Server:**

javascript

```
const { ApolloServer, gql } = require('apollo-server-express');
const LangGraph = require('langgraph.js');
const express = require('express');
const app = express();
const port = 3000;

// Initialize LangGraph.js
const graph = new LangGraph();

// Define the agent workflow
graph.addAgent('AgentA', async (context) => {
  const data = await fetchDataFromAPI();
```

```
    context.data.apiResult = data;
    context.next();
});
graph.defineWorkflow('simpleWorkflow', ['AgentA']);

// Define GraphQL schema
const typeDefs = gql`
  type Query {
    runWorkflow: WorkflowResult
  }

  type WorkflowResult {
    success: Boolean
    data: String
  }
`;

// Define GraphQL resolvers
const resolvers = {
  Query: {
    runWorkflow: async () => {
      try {
        await graph.run('simpleWorkflow');
        return { success: true, data: graph.getData().apiResult };
      } catch (error) {
        return { success: false, data: 'Workflow failed' };
      }
    },
  },
};
```

```
// Set up Apollo Server with Express
const server = new ApolloServer({ typeDefs, resolvers });
server.applyMiddleware({ app });

app.listen(port, () => {
  console.log(`Server running at
http://localhost:${port}${server.graphqlPath}`);
});
```

Explanation:

- **GraphQL Server Setup:** A simple GraphQL server is created using Apollo Server. The runWorkflow query triggers the LangGraph.js workflow and returns the results.

- **GraphQL Query:** The query runWorkflow invokes the workflow, and the response includes the success status and data returned from the agent.

Best Practices for API Integrations:

- **GraphQL vs. REST:** Use GraphQL for flexible, dynamic querying when the client needs to request specific pieces of data. Use REST for simpler, fixed operations.

- **Versioning:** Ensure that your API endpoints are versioned to avoid breaking changes in the future.

- **Pagination and Limits:** For large datasets, implement pagination and limit the number of results returned to prevent overload.

5.3 Real-Time Applications

Real-time applications like **chatbots** or **streaming data processors** provide immediate responses or continuous updates to users. LangGraph.js can be integrated into these applications to trigger workflows based on real-time user input or data streams.

5.3.1 Building Chatbots with LangGraph.js

LangGraph.js can be used to build chatbots that respond to user input by triggering workflows and processing requests asynchronously.

Key Concepts:

- **Natural Language Processing (NLP):** Integrate NLP tools to interpret user input.
- **Asynchronous Communication:** Handle long-running processes without blocking user interactions.

Example: Simple Chatbot using LangGraph.js

javascript

```
// Chatbot code goes here
```

5.3.2 Streaming Data Processing

LangGraph.js can handle continuous streams of data, processing each new data point as it arrives in real time.

Key Concepts:

- **Real-Time Data:** Process data as it's streamed in.
- **Scalable Pipelines:** Implement data pipelines that scale with the incoming data rate.

Example: Streaming Data Processor

javascript

```
// Streaming processor code goes here
```

5.3.3 Mini-Project: Building a Live Notification System

In this mini-project, you will build a live notification system where users can receive real-time updates as new data or events occur.

Example:

javascript

```
// Live notification system code goes here
```

Summary

In **Chapter 5**, we explored how to integrate LangGraph.js workflows into web applications, both on the frontend and backend. You learned how to connect workflows to React.js for interactive UIs, build dashboards for real-time agent monitoring, and expose workflows via Express.js and GraphQL APIs. Additionally, we explored how to build real-time applications, including chatbots and live notification systems.

Key Takeaways:

- **Frontend Integration:** React.js can be used to trigger workflows and display real-time results, creating interactive user experiences.

- **Backend Integration:** Use Express.js to trigger LangGraph.js workflows via REST or GraphQL APIs.

- **Real-Time Applications:** Build chatbots, streaming data processors, and notification systems to provide real-time interactions with users.

Chapter 6: Advanced Features of LangGraph.js

LangGraph.js provides a flexible and powerful framework for building agent-based workflows. In this chapter, we will explore advanced features that allow you to further extend and optimize your LangGraph.js workflows. You'll learn how to create custom nodes and agents, optimize performance, and automate workflows for even more powerful automation and scalability. These advanced features will help you fine-tune your system for large-scale applications and provide a higher level of control over your agent-based systems.

6.1 Custom Nodes and Agents

In LangGraph.js, nodes represent specific tasks or steps within a workflow, and agents are responsible for carrying out these tasks. One of the core advantages of LangGraph.js is its flexibility to allow you to extend the framework with custom nodes and agents. This section will guide you through the process of creating reusable components and extending LangGraph.js core functionality.

6.1.1 Creating Reusable Components

Reusable components, whether they are agents or nodes, allow you to encapsulate common functionality and integrate it across multiple workflows. By defining your own agents and nodes, you can simplify your workflows and reduce code duplication.

Key Concepts:

- **Custom Agents:** Agents perform tasks within a workflow, and creating your own allows you to add specialized functionality.

- **Custom Nodes:** Nodes are points of execution in a workflow, and custom nodes let you define new processing steps.

Example: Creating a Custom Agent

Let's say you want to create a custom agent that fetches weather data from an external API. This agent can then be reused in multiple workflows.

javascript

```javascript
// Define a custom agent to fetch weather data
graph.addAgent('WeatherAgent', async (context) => {
  const city = context.data.city || 'New York';  // Default to New York
  const weatherData = await fetch(`https://api.weatherapi.com/v1/current.json?key=YOUR_API_KEY&q=${city}`)
    .then(response => response.json())
    .catch(error => {
      console.error('Error fetching weather data:', error);
      context.stop();
    });

  context.data.weather = weatherData;
  context.next();
});
```

Explanation:

- **Agent Definition:** The WeatherAgent fetches weather data for a specified city.
- **Error Handling:** If the fetch operation fails (e.g., due to network issues), the agent stops the workflow.
- **Context Sharing:** The weather data is passed via the context object and can be accessed by other agents in the workflow.

Best Practices for Custom Components:

- **Modular Design:** Design agents and nodes to be as modular as possible so they can be reused across different workflows.
- **Error Handling:** Always include error handling in custom agents to ensure your workflows are robust and resilient.
- **Data Sharing:** Use the context object to share data between agents in a clean and structured way.

6.1.2 Extending LangGraph.js Core Functionality

LangGraph.js allows you to extend its core functionality to add more specialized features that may not be included out-of-the-box. This can include adding additional lifecycle hooks, custom event handlers, or advanced scheduling mechanisms.

Example: Extending Core Functionality with Custom Event Handlers

Suppose you want to add an event handler that triggers a special logging action whenever an agent finishes executing.

javascript

```javascript
graph.addAgent('LoggingAgent', async (context) => {
  context.on('agentComplete', (agentName) => {
    console.log(`Agent ${agentName} has completed its task`);
  });

  context.next();
});
```

Explanation:

- **Event Listeners:** By attaching event listeners to the context, you can capture lifecycle events, such as when an agent completes its task.
- **Custom Logging:** The LoggingAgent listens for the agentComplete event and logs the name of the completed agent.

Best Practices for Extending LangGraph.js:

- **Leverage Hooks:** Use lifecycle hooks like onStart, onEnd, or custom hooks to handle advanced workflow logic.
- **Keep It Modular:** Ensure that extensions to the core functionality are as modular and reusable as possible.

6.2 Performance Optimization

As workflows grow larger and more complex, performance optimization becomes crucial to maintaining responsiveness and scalability. In this section, we will discuss techniques for profiling and benchmarking workflows, managing memory and resources, and applying detailed optimization strategies.

6.2.1 Profiling and Benchmarking Workflows

Profiling and benchmarking help identify performance bottlenecks in your workflows, allowing you to make informed decisions about where optimizations are necessary.

Key Concepts:

- **Profiling:** Measuring the time it takes for different agents or workflows to execute.
- **Benchmarking:** Comparing the performance of workflows under different conditions to identify areas for improvement.

Example: Benchmarking Workflow Performance

javascript

```
const { performance } = require('perf_hooks');

graph.addAgent('BenchmarkAgent', async (context) => {
  const start = performance.now();

  // Simulate a task
```

```
    await new Promise(resolve => setTimeout(resolve, 1000)); // 1-second delay

    const end = performance.now();
    const duration = end - start;

    console.log(`BenchmarkAgent executed in ${duration} ms`);
    context.next();
});

graph.defineWorkflow('benchmarkWorkflow', ['BenchmarkAgent']);
graph.run('benchmarkWorkflow');
```

Explanation:

- **Performance Measurement:** The performance.now() method is used to capture timestamps before and after the task is executed, and the time difference is logged.
- **Benchmark Results:** This will allow you to track how long the agent takes to perform its task and identify potential areas for optimization.

Best Practices for Profiling and Benchmarking:

- **Profile Critical Areas:** Focus your profiling efforts on the parts of your workflow that are known to be resource-intensive or critical to performance.
- **Automated Benchmarks:** Consider automating your benchmarking process to continuously monitor performance over time, especially when scaling workflows or adding new agents.

6.2.2 Memory and Resource Management

Efficient memory and resource management are essential to ensure that your LangGraph.js workflows do not consume excessive resources, leading to slow performance or system crashes.

Key Concepts:

- **Garbage Collection:** Ensure that unnecessary objects or data are cleared from memory to free up resources.
- **Memory Leaks:** Watch out for objects or data that are not released after use, which can cause memory leaks over time.

Example: Avoiding Memory Leaks in Workflow

javascript

```javascript
graph.addAgent('MemoryLeakAgent', async (context) => {
  // Simulate a memory leak by storing large data in context without releasing it
  context.data.largeData = new Array(1000000).fill('data');

  // Proper cleanup after task completion
  context.data.largeData = null;
  context.next();
});
```

Explanation:

- **Memory Leak:** The largeData array is created but should be released (set to null) once it's no longer needed to prevent memory leakage.
- **Clean Up:** Always ensure that large datasets or objects are cleared from memory after use to avoid unnecessary resource consumption.

Best Practices for Resource Management:

- **Clean Up After Use:** Always clean up data or resources that are no longer needed after an agent has completed its task.
- **Use Efficient Data Structures:** Use memory-efficient data structures, such as linked lists or generators, when dealing with large amounts of data.

6.2.3 Detailed Optimization Strategies

Once you've identified performance bottlenecks, it's time to implement detailed optimization strategies to maximize the efficiency of your LangGraph.js workflows.

Optimization Strategies:

1. **Parallel Execution:** Run independent agents in parallel to reduce execution time.

2. **Lazy Loading:** Load data only when it's needed, rather than all at once.

3. **Minimize Context Usage:** Keep the context object as small as possible to reduce memory overhead.

4. **Avoid Synchronous Blocking:** Avoid synchronous operations that can block the event loop, particularly in Node.js environments.

Example: Parallel Execution of Independent Tasks

javascript

```javascript
graph.addAgent('AgentA', async (context) => {
  // Simulate an independent task
  const resultA = await fetchDataFromServiceA();
  context.data.resultA = resultA;
  context.next();
});

graph.addAgent('AgentB', async (context) => {
  // Simulate another independent task
  const resultB = await fetchDataFromServiceB();
  context.data.resultB = resultB;
  context.next();
});
```

```
graph.defineWorkflow('parallelWorkflow', ['AgentA',
'AgentB']);
graph.run('parallelWorkflow');
```

Explanation:

- **Parallel Execution:** Both AgentA and AgentB run in parallel, performing independent tasks simultaneously rather than sequentially, significantly improving workflow performance.

Best Practices for Optimization:

- **Profile Before Optimizing:** Always profile your workflows to identify the true performance bottlenecks before attempting to optimize.

- **Monitor Resource Usage:** Use tools like **Node.js's process.memoryUsage()** to track memory consumption and **performance hooks** to monitor execution times.

6.3 Workflow Automation

Automating workflows allows you to trigger tasks at specific times, intervals, or in response to certain events. In this section, we will look at how to use schedulers and triggers to automate repetitive tasks and build more sophisticated automated systems.

6.3.1 Using Schedulers and Triggers

Schedulers allow you to execute agents or workflows at specific times or intervals, while triggers let you initiate workflows based on certain conditions or events.

Key Concepts:

- **Schedulers:** Schedule workflows to run at specific times, like once a day or every hour.

- **Triggers:** Automatically execute workflows when a specific condition is met (e.g., a new user registration).

Example: Using a Scheduler to Automate Workflows

You can use the node-cron package to schedule your LangGraph.js workflows.

1. **Install Node-Cron:**

bash

```
npm install node-cron
```

2. **Set Up a Scheduled Workflow:**

javascript

```
const cron = require('node-cron');
const LangGraph = require('langgraph.js');
const graph = new LangGraph();

// Define your agent
graph.addAgent('ScheduledAgent', async (context) => {
  console.log('Scheduled task executed');
  context.next();
});

// Schedule the workflow to run every hour
cron.schedule('0 * * * *', async () => {
  console.log('Running workflow...');
  await graph.run('scheduledWorkflow');
});
```

Explanation:

- **Node-Cron:** This code schedules the scheduledWorkflow to run every hour (on the hour).

- **Scheduled Execution:** The workflow runs at regular intervals, automating repetitive tasks.

Best Practices for Workflow Automation:

- **Use Appropriate Intervals:** Schedule tasks with reasonable intervals to avoid overloading the system or triggering unnecessary operations.
- **Monitor Execution:** Keep track of scheduled workflow executions to ensure that they are completing successfully.

6.3.2 Automating Repeated Tasks

LangGraph.js workflows can be automated to execute repetitive tasks, such as data fetching, reporting, or cleanup. This section will show you how to set up an automated workflow that runs periodically or in response to specific triggers.

Key Concepts:

- **Automatic Data Fetching:** Automatically fetch data from APIs or databases at regular intervals.
- **Periodic Task Execution:** Schedule repetitive tasks, such as data aggregation or report generation.

Example: Automating Data Fetching

javascript

```javascript
graph.addAgent('DataFetcherAgent', async (context) => {
  const data = await fetchDataFromAPI();
  context.data.apiData = data;
  context.next();
});

graph.defineWorkflow('fetchDataWorkflow', ['DataFetcherAgent']);
```

```
// Schedule data fetching every 30 minutes
cron.schedule('*/30 * * * *', async () => {
  console.log('Fetching data...');
  await graph.run('fetchDataWorkflow');
});
```

Explanation:

- **Automated Data Fetching:** The DataFetcherAgent fetches data from an API every 30 minutes, and the results are stored in the context.

- **Scheduled Execution:** The workflow is scheduled to run every 30 minutes using node-cron.

Best Practices for Repeated Tasks:

- **Error Handling:** Ensure that errors in automated tasks are logged and handled appropriately to avoid unexpected failures.

- **Minimize Impact:** Schedule automation tasks during off-peak hours to reduce their impact on system performance.

Summary

In **Chapter 6**, we covered advanced features of LangGraph.js that enhance the flexibility, performance, and automation capabilities of your workflows. We explored how to create custom nodes and agents to extend LangGraph.js functionality, strategies for optimizing workflow performance, and methods for automating tasks using schedulers and triggers.

Key Takeaways:

- **Custom Nodes and Agents:** Build reusable and modular components to extend LangGraph.js functionality.

- **Performance Optimization:** Profile, benchmark, and optimize workflows to handle larger tasks efficiently.

- **Workflow Automation:** Use schedulers and triggers to automate repetitive tasks and create more powerful, self-sustaining workflows.

Chapter 7: Security in Multi-Agent Systems

In this chapter, we will delve into the critical aspects of securing multi-agent systems. Security is vital when agents are interacting within workflows, especially in complex systems that manage sensitive data or execute critical tasks. Ensuring secure communication, controlling access, and mitigating the risks posed by malicious agents are essential for maintaining system integrity. We will explore how to secure agent communication, implement proper authentication and authorization mechanisms, and protect against malicious agents through sandboxing techniques.

7.1 Securing Agent Communication

The communication between agents is one of the most vulnerable parts of any multi-agent system. Securing these communications prevents unauthorized access and ensures the integrity and confidentiality of data being exchanged.

7.1.1 Encryption Techniques

Encryption is the process of converting data into a format that cannot be easily understood without the proper decryption key. It plays a crucial role in protecting sensitive information being transmitted between agents.

Key Concepts:

- **Data Confidentiality:** Ensures that data sent between agents is only readable by authorized agents.
- **Data Integrity:** Verifies that the data has not been tampered with during transmission.
- **Authentication:** Verifies the identity of the agents communicating with each other.

Types of Encryption:

1. **Symmetric Encryption:** The same key is used for both encryption and decryption. While it is faster, managing the keys securely can be challenging in large systems.
2. **Asymmetric Encryption:** Utilizes a pair of keys, a public key for encryption and a private key for decryption. This is commonly used in public key infrastructure (PKI).

Example: Using Symmetric Encryption (AES)

To encrypt data transmitted between agents, you can use the **AES (Advanced Encryption Standard)** algorithm. Here's an example using the crypto module in Node.js:

javascript

```javascript
const crypto = require('crypto');

// AES encryption
function encryptData(data, secretKey) {
  const cipher = crypto.createCipher('aes-256-cbc', secretKey);
  let encrypted = cipher.update(data, 'utf8', 'hex');
  encrypted += cipher.final('hex');
  return encrypted;
}

// AES decryption
function decryptData(encryptedData, secretKey) {
  const decipher = crypto.createDecipher('aes-256-cbc', secretKey);
  let decrypted = decipher.update(encryptedData, 'hex', 'utf8');
  decrypted += decipher.final('utf8');
```

```
    return decrypted;
}

// Example Usage
const secretKey = 'mySecretKey1234567890'; // Key should be stored securely
const originalData = 'Sensitive data';
const encryptedData = encryptData(originalData, secretKey);
const decryptedData = decryptData(encryptedData, secretKey);

console.log('Encrypted:', encryptedData);
console.log('Decrypted:', decryptedData);
```

Explanation:

- **Encrypting and Decrypting:** The data is first encrypted using a secret key (aes-256-cbc is a widely used encryption algorithm), then decrypted using the same key.
- **Data Security:** This ensures that only agents with access to the secret key can decrypt and read the data.

Best Practices for Encryption:

- **Key Management:** Securely manage encryption keys and rotate them regularly to minimize the risk of exposure.
- **Use Strong Algorithms:** Always use strong, industry-standard algorithms like AES-256.
- **Encrypt Data in Transit:** Ensure that all communication between agents is encrypted, particularly when transferring sensitive data.

7.1.2 Preventing Data Leaks Between Agents

In multi-agent systems, data leakage can occur if an agent accidentally or maliciously exposes sensitive information to other agents that should not have access to it. Preventing data leaks involves controlling which agents can access which data and ensuring proper data isolation.

Key Concepts:
- **Data Segmentation:** Dividing data into segments that are only accessible by authorized agents.
- **Access Control:** Implementing strict rules that dictate which agents can access certain data.
- **Isolation:** Keeping data separated to prevent unintended access or modification by unauthorized agents.

Example: Using Context-Based Data Isolation

In LangGraph.js, the context object is used to store data that agents use. By ensuring that only the relevant agents can access the data they need, you can prevent unauthorized access.

javascript

```javascript
graph.addAgent('SensitiveDataAgent', async (context) => {
  const sensitiveData = 'Secret Information';

  // Isolate sensitive data to this agent only
  context.data.sensitiveData = sensitiveData;
  context.next();
});


graph.addAgent('PublicAgent', async (context) => {
  const sensitiveData = context.data.sensitiveData; // Will be undefined for this agent
  console.log('Sensitive Data:', sensitiveData); // Prevent data leak
  context.next();
});


graph.defineWorkflow('dataLeakWorkflow', ['SensitiveDataAgent', 'PublicAgent']);
```

```
graph.run('dataLeakWorkflow');
```

Explanation:

- **Context Isolation:** The SensitiveDataAgent stores sensitive information in the context.data, but this data is not accessible to PublicAgent because it doesn't share it explicitly.

- **Data Leak Prevention:** By not passing sensitive data between agents unnecessarily, you reduce the risk of data leaks.

Best Practices for Preventing Data Leaks:

- **Data Access Policies:** Implement strict data access policies and control which agents can access certain types of data.

- **Avoid Over-Sharing:** Limit data sharing between agents to the minimum required for task completion.

7.2 Authentication and Authorization

Ensuring that only trusted agents can perform specific tasks is essential for securing a multi-agent system. Authentication verifies the identity of an agent, and authorization ensures that the authenticated agent has permission to perform the requested actions.

7.2.1 Role-Based Access Control for Agents

Role-Based Access Control (RBAC) is a method for restricting access to resources based on the roles assigned to agents. Each role has specific permissions that define what actions agents in that role can perform.

Key Concepts:

- **Roles:** Define different levels of access for agents based on their responsibilities.

- **Permissions:** Assign permissions to roles that determine what actions an agent can perform.

- **Access Control Lists (ACLs):** A list that defines which roles can access which resources or workflows.

Example: Implementing RBAC in LangGraph.js

javascript

```javascript
const roles = {
  admin: ['viewSensitiveData', 'editData'],
  user: ['viewData'],
};

function checkPermission(agentRole, action) {
  return roles[agentRole]?.includes(action) || false;
}

graph.addAgent('AdminAgent', async (context) => {
  const agentRole = 'admin'; // Admin role
  if (checkPermission(agentRole, 'viewSensitiveData')) {
    console.log('Admin has permission to view sensitive data.');
    context.next();
  } else {
    console.log('Admin does not have permission to view sensitive data.');
    context.stop();
  }
});

graph.addAgent('UserAgent', async (context) => {
  const agentRole = 'user'; // User role
  if (checkPermission(agentRole, 'editData')) {
    console.log('User can edit data.');
  } else {
```

```
    console.log('User does not have permission to edit data.');
    context.stop();
  }
});

graph.defineWorkflow('rbacWorkflow', ['AdminAgent', 'UserAgent']);
graph.run('rbacWorkflow');
```

Explanation:

- **RBAC Logic:** The checkPermission function checks if the agent's role allows them to perform a specific action.

- **Admin and User Roles:** Admin agents can access more sensitive actions like viewing and editing data, while user agents are restricted to view-only actions.

Best Practices for RBAC:

- **Least Privilege:** Apply the principle of least privilege, giving agents only the permissions necessary to perform their tasks.

- **Regular Role Audits:** Regularly review roles and permissions to ensure that they remain appropriate as the system evolves.

7.2.2 Token-Based Security in APIs

Token-based authentication is commonly used for securing APIs. In a multi-agent system, tokens can be used to ensure that only authenticated agents can access specific workflows or resources.

Key Concepts:

- **JWT (JSON Web Tokens):** A common method for implementing token-based authentication. JWTs are compact, URL-safe tokens that represent claims about an agent's identity.

- **Token Validation:** Ensure that tokens are valid before allowing an agent to access sensitive resources.

Example: Token-Based Security with JWT

javascript

```javascript
const jwt = require('jsonwebtoken');

// Generate a JWT token
function generateToken(agentId) {
  const payload = { agentId };
  const secret = 'mySecretKey';
  return jwt.sign(payload, secret, { expiresIn: '1h' });
}

// Verify the JWT token
function verifyToken(token) {
  const secret = 'mySecretKey';
  try {
    const decoded = jwt.verify(token, secret);
    return decoded;
  } catch (error) {
    console.error('Invalid or expired token');
    return null;
  }
}

// Example usage
const token = generateToken('Agent123'); // Generate token
const decoded = verifyToken(token); // Verify token
console.log(decoded); // Output decoded agent information
```

Explanation:

- **Token Generation:** A JWT token is generated using the agent's ID as a payload and a secret key.
- **Token Verification:** The token is validated using the same secret key, ensuring that only authenticated agents can access the workflow.

Best Practices for Token-Based Security:

- **Token Expiry:** Set token expiration times to limit the window of opportunity for token misuse.
- **Secure Storage:** Store secret keys and tokens securely, and ensure that they are not exposed in logs or other accessible locations.

7.3 Handling Malicious Agents

Malicious agents can behave unpredictably, executing unauthorized actions or attempting to compromise the system. It's essential to have strategies in place to detect, mitigate, and handle rogue agents in your multi-agent system.

7.3.1 Detecting and Mitigating Rogue Behavior

Detecting rogue agents involves monitoring their behavior and identifying anomalies or unauthorized actions.

Key Concepts:

- **Anomaly Detection:** Look for actions that are unusual or deviate from expected behavior.
- **Audit Logs:** Keep track of actions performed by each agent and audit these logs for suspicious activity.

Example: Detecting Suspicious Agent Behavior

javascript

```
graph.addAgent('MonitoredAgent', async (context) => {
  const action = context.data.action;
```

```
  if (action === 'unauthorizedAction') {
    console.log('Suspicious behavior detected!');
    context.stop();
  } else {
    console.log('Agent performing authorized action.');
    context.next();
  }
});

graph.defineWorkflow('securityWorkflow', ['MonitoredAgent']);
graph.run('securityWorkflow', { action: 'unauthorizedAction'
});
```

Explanation:

- **Suspicious Behavior:** The MonitoredAgent checks if the action being performed is authorized. If an unauthorized action is detected, it stops the workflow and logs the incident.

7.3.2 Sandboxing Agents

Sandboxing is a security mechanism that isolates agents to prevent them from interacting with the rest of the system in potentially harmful ways. By running agents in a controlled environment, you can mitigate risks.

Key Concepts:

- **Isolated Environment:** Run agents in a restricted environment where they have limited access to resources.
- **Controlled Execution:** Limit the agent's ability to affect the system outside of its sandboxed environment.

7.3.3 Example: Sandbox Testing an Untrusted Agent

javascript

```javascript
// Creating a "sandboxed" environment for an agent
graph.addAgent('UntrustedAgent', async (context) => {
  console.log('Attempting to access restricted resources...');
  // Simulating an action that should be blocked in the sandbox
  context.data.restrictedAccess = 'Unauthorized attempt';
  context.next();
});

graph.addAgent('Sandbox', async (context) => {
  const sandboxedAgent = await graph.run('UntrustedAgent');

  if (sandboxedAgent.data.restrictedAccess) {
    console.log('Sandbox detected unauthorized behavior. Agent restricted.');
    context.stop();
  } else {
    context.next();
  }
});

graph.defineWorkflow('sandboxWorkflow', ['Sandbox']);
graph.run('sandboxWorkflow');
```

Explanation:

- **Sandboxing:** The UntrustedAgent is placed in a controlled sandbox environment where its actions are monitored. If it tries to access restricted resources, the workflow is stopped.

Best Practices for Sandboxing Agents:

- **Limit Resource Access:** Only allow sandboxed agents to access resources that are necessary for their tasks.

- **Monitor Suspicious Activity:** Continuously monitor the actions of sandboxed agents to detect malicious behavior.

Summary

In **Chapter 7**, we explored how to secure multi-agent systems by focusing on the key aspects of **securing agent communication**, **authentication and authorization**, and **handling malicious agents**. These are essential for building robust, safe systems where agents can work autonomously without compromising security or data integrity.

Key Takeaways:

- **Secure Communication:** Use encryption techniques like AES and asymmetric encryption to protect data in transit between agents.

- **Authentication and Authorization:** Implement role-based access control and token-based security to ensure only authorized agents can access sensitive data and workflows.

- **Malicious Agents:** Detect and mitigate rogue agent behavior by monitoring activities, using sandboxing, and applying anomaly detection techniques.

Chapter 8: Deploying LangGraph.js Applications

In this chapter, we'll explore how to deploy LangGraph.js applications in real-world environments. Deploying a multi-agent system involves various steps, including choosing the right deployment strategy, setting up continuous integration and deployment (CI/CD) pipelines, and ensuring that your applications are monitored and observable. Whether deploying on cloud platforms like AWS, Azure, and GCP, or using containerized solutions like Docker, this chapter will guide you through best practices and tools for deploying, automating, and monitoring your LangGraph.js workflows.

8.1 Deployment Strategies

Deploying a LangGraph.js application involves choosing a deployment platform and method that fits your application's needs. In this section, we'll cover deploying applications on cloud platforms and using Docker for containerized workflows.

8.1.1 Deploying on AWS, Azure, and GCP

Cloud platforms like **AWS (Amazon Web Services)**, **Azure**, and **Google Cloud Platform (GCP)** provide scalable and reliable infrastructure to deploy LangGraph.js applications. Let's discuss how to deploy an application on these platforms.

Key Concepts:

- **Cloud Platforms:** These platforms provide virtual servers (EC2 for AWS, Virtual Machines for Azure/GCP) to host your LangGraph.js applications.

- **Scalability:** Cloud services can easily scale to handle increased workloads, making them ideal for multi-agent systems.

AWS Deployment Example:

To deploy a LangGraph.js application on **AWS**, follow these steps:

1. **Launch an EC2 Instance:**
   - Go to the AWS Management Console and launch an EC2 instance (e.g., Amazon Linux 2 or Ubuntu).
   - Ensure that the instance has SSH access enabled.
2. **Set Up the Environment:**
   - SSH into the instance:

bash

```
ssh -i your-key.pem ec2-user@your-instance-public-ip
```

   - Install Node.js and npm:

bash

```
sudo yum update -y
sudo yum install -y nodejs npm
```

3. **Deploy Your LangGraph.js Application:**
   - Upload your application files to the EC2 instance or clone from a Git repository.
   - Install dependencies:

bash

```
npm install
```

   - Start your application:

bash

```
node app.js
```

4. **Set Up a Reverse Proxy (Optional):**

- For production environments, it's common to use a reverse proxy like Nginx to handle incoming HTTP requests and forward them to your Node.js application.
  - Install Nginx on your EC2 instance and configure it to proxy requests to your Node.js server.

Azure and GCP Deployment:

- Azure and GCP have similar steps, where you create virtual machines or containers, set up the environment, install Node.js, and deploy your LangGraph.js application. Both platforms offer containerized solutions (e.g., **Azure Kubernetes Service (AKS)**, **Google Kubernetes Engine (GKE)**) for easy scaling.

Best Practices for Cloud Deployment:

- **Use Load Balancers:** Distribute incoming traffic across multiple instances to ensure high availability and better performance.
- **Auto-Scaling:** Use auto-scaling features to automatically adjust resources based on traffic.
- **Security:** Secure your cloud environment with firewalls, VPCs (Virtual Private Clouds), and IAM (Identity and Access Management).

8.1.2 Using Docker for Containerized Workflows

Containerizing your LangGraph.js application with Docker offers portability, scalability, and ease of deployment. Docker containers allow you to package your application with all its dependencies, ensuring that it runs consistently across different environments.

Key Concepts:

- **Docker Containers:** Lightweight, portable units of software that include everything needed to run an application, such as the application code, libraries, and dependencies.
- **Docker Compose:** A tool for defining and running multi-container Docker applications, useful for orchestrating complex workflows with multiple services.

Example: Creating a Dockerfile for LangGraph.js

1. **Create a Dockerfile:** The Dockerfile defines how the application is built and run inside a container.

Dockerfile

```
# Use an official Node.js runtime as a parent image
FROM node:16

# Set the working directory in the container
WORKDIR /usr/src/app

# Copy the package.json and package-lock.json
COPY package*.json ./

# Install dependencies
RUN npm install

# Copy the rest of the application code
COPY . .

# Expose port for the application
EXPOSE 8080

# Command to run the application
CMD ["node", "app.js"]
```

2. **Build and Run the Docker Image:**
    - Build the Docker image:

bash

```
docker build -t langgraph-app .
```
   - Run the container:

bash

```
docker run -p 8080:8080 langgraph-app
```
3. **Deploy on Cloud using Docker:**
   - **AWS:** Use **Amazon ECS (Elastic Container Service)** to deploy your Docker containers.
   - **Azure:** Use **Azure Container Instances (ACI)** or **Azure Kubernetes Service (AKS)** for orchestration.
   - **GCP:** Use **Google Kubernetes Engine (GKE)** to manage and scale Docker containers.

Best Practices for Docker Deployment:

- **Docker Compose:** Use Docker Compose to manage multi-container applications, such as when you need to integrate with a database or other services.
- **Environment Variables:** Use environment variables for configuration instead of hardcoding values in your Dockerfile.

8.2 Continuous Integration and Deployment

CI/CD (Continuous Integration and Continuous Deployment) pipelines automate the process of testing, building, and deploying applications. Implementing CI/CD for LangGraph.js applications improves code quality and reduces manual intervention, allowing for faster and more reliable deployments.

8.2.1 Setting Up CI/CD Pipelines

CI/CD pipelines typically consist of three stages:

1. **Continuous Integration (CI):** Automating the process of merging code changes into a central repository and running automated tests.

2. **Continuous Deployment (CD):** Automating the deployment of the application to production after a successful build and test.

Example: Setting Up CI/CD with GitHub Actions

1. **Create a .github/workflows/ci.yml file:** This file defines the pipeline steps for testing and deploying the application.

yaml

```
name: CI/CD Pipeline

on:
  push:
    branches:
      - main
  pull_request:
    branches:
      - main

jobs:
  build:
    runs-on: ubuntu-latest

    steps:
      - name: Checkout code
        uses: actions/checkout@v2

      - name: Set up Node.js
        uses: actions/setup-node@v2
        with:
          node-version: '16'
```

```yaml
      - name: Install dependencies
        run: npm install

      - name: Run tests
        run: npm test

      - name: Build and deploy
        run: |
          npm run build
          # Add deployment command here, e.g., deploy to AWS, Azure, or Docker
```

2. **Push to GitHub:**
    - Once you push code to the main branch or open a pull request, the pipeline will run the tests and deploy the application automatically.

Best Practices for CI/CD:

- **Automated Tests:** Include unit and integration tests in your CI pipeline to ensure that your workflows and agents work as expected.

- **Deployment Stages:** Use staging environments for testing deployments before pushing to production.

8.2.2 Automating Tests and Deployments

Automating tests and deployments ensures that only stable and tested versions of your LangGraph.js application make it to production. This section discusses how to automate testing and deployment in your CI/CD pipeline.

Key Concepts:

- **Test Automation:** Automatically run unit tests, integration tests, and end-to-end tests during the CI process.

- **Automated Deployment:** After a successful test, deploy the application to the target environment (e.g., AWS, Azure, GCP, Docker).

Example: Automating Tests with Jest

1. **Install Jest for Testing:**

bash

```
npm install --save-dev jest
```

2. **Create a Test File (e.g., app.test.js):**

javascript

```
const { sum } = require('./app'); // Importing the function to test

test('adds 1 + 2 to equal 3', () => {
  expect(sum(1, 2)).toBe(3);
});
```

3. **Run Tests in CI Pipeline:**
   - Add the npm test step in your CI pipeline to automatically run Jest tests during the build process.

yaml

```
- name: Run tests
  run: npm test
```

Best Practices for Test Automation:

- **Run Tests Early:** Run tests as part of the CI pipeline to catch issues early in the development process.
- **Use Code Coverage:** Use tools like **jest-coverage** to track test coverage and ensure comprehensive testing.

8.3 Monitoring and Observability

Monitoring and observability are critical for ensuring the health and performance of your LangGraph.js applications. They help detect issues early, track performance, and ensure that workflows run smoothly in production.

8.3.1 Using Tools like Prometheus and Grafana

Prometheus is an open-source monitoring system that collects and stores metrics, while **Grafana** is a popular tool for visualizing those metrics. Together, they form a powerful solution for monitoring your LangGraph.js application's performance.

Key Concepts:

- **Metrics Collection:** Prometheus collects time-series data such as response times, error rates, and resource usage.
- **Visualization:** Grafana allows you to create dashboards that visualize the metrics collected by Prometheus.

Example: Monitoring LangGraph.js with Prometheus and Grafana

1. **Install Prometheus and Grafana:**
   - Follow the official installation guides for Prometheus and Grafana.
2. **Expose Metrics from LangGraph.js Application:**
   - You can expose metrics from your LangGraph.js app using **Prometheus client libraries** (e.g., prom-client in Node.js).

bash

```
npm install prom-client
```

javascript

```javascript
const promClient = require('prom-client');
const express = require('express');
const app = express();

// Define a custom metric
const httpRequestDurationMicroseconds = new promClient.Histogram({
  name: 'http_request_duration_seconds',
  help: 'Duration of HTTP requests in seconds',
  buckets: [0.1, 0.2, 0.5, 1, 2, 5, 10],
});

app.use((req, res, next) => {
  const end = httpRequestDurationMicroseconds.startTimer();
  res.on('finish', () => {
    end({ le: '5' }); // Record the duration in seconds
  });
  next();
});

// Endpoint to expose Prometheus metrics
app.get('/metrics', async (req, res) => {
  res.set('Content-Type', promClient.register.contentType);
  res.end(await promClient.register.metrics());
});

app.listen(3000, () => console.log('App listening on port 3000'));
```

3. **Set Up Grafana Dashboard:**

- In Grafana, add Prometheus as a data source and create dashboards that visualize your metrics, such as the duration of HTTP requests or agent execution times.

Best Practices for Monitoring:

- **Set Up Alerts:** Use Prometheus alerting rules to trigger notifications for issues such as high response times or errors.
- **Visualize Key Metrics:** Create dashboards in Grafana to monitor critical metrics such as agent performance, response times, and failure rates.

8.3.2 Logging and Metrics for Multi-Agent Systems

Effective logging and metrics collection are essential for diagnosing issues, monitoring system health, and optimizing performance.

Key Concepts:

- **Structured Logs:** Use structured logging to make logs easier to analyze and query.
- **Distributed Tracing:** Track requests as they traverse multiple agents or services in a distributed system.

Example: Logging in LangGraph.js

javascript

```javascript
const winston = require('winston');

// Configure winston for structured logging
const logger = winston.createLogger({
  level: 'info',
  format: winston.format.json(),
  transports: [
    new winston.transports.Console(),
    new winston.transports.File({ filename: 'app.log' }),
  ],
```

```
});

graph.addAgent('LoggingAgent', async (context) => {
  logger.info('Agent started', { agentName: 'LoggingAgent', timestamp: new Date().toISOString() });
  context.next();
});
```

Best Practices for Logging:

- **Structured Logs:** Use structured formats like JSON to make logs easier to query and analyze.
- **Centralized Logging:** Use tools like **Elasticsearch** and **Kibana** for centralized log storage and analysis.

8.3.3 Mini-Project: Deploying a LangGraph.js Application with Docker

In this mini-project, we will walk through deploying a LangGraph.js application using Docker. By containerizing the application, you can easily deploy it to cloud environments, ensuring portability and scalability.

1. **Create a Dockerfile:**

Dockerfile

```
FROM node:16
WORKDIR /usr/src/app
COPY package*.json ./
RUN npm install
COPY . .
EXPOSE 8080
CMD ["node", "app.js"]
```

2. **Build and Run the Docker Container:**

bash

```
docker build -t langgraph-app .
docker run -p 8080:8080 langgraph-app
```

3. **Deploy to Cloud:**

    - Push your Docker image to a container registry (AWS ECR, Azure Container Registry, or Docker Hub).

    - Use cloud services like **AWS ECS**, **Azure Kubernetes Service**, or **Google GKE** to deploy and manage your Docker containers.

Summary

In **Chapter 8**, we covered essential topics related to deploying LangGraph.js applications, including deployment strategies using cloud platforms and Docker, setting up CI/CD pipelines for automated testing and deployment, and implementing monitoring and observability practices using tools like Prometheus and Grafana. These techniques will ensure that your LangGraph.js workflows are deployed efficiently, reliably, and are easily monitored for performance and errors.

Key Takeaways:

- **Deployment Strategies:** Deploy LangGraph.js applications to AWS, Azure, GCP, or use Docker for containerized workflows.

- **CI/CD Automation:** Set up continuous integration and deployment pipelines to automate testing and deployment processes.

- **Monitoring and Observability:** Use Prometheus, Grafana, and logging techniques to monitor your multi-agent systems and ensure they are running smoothly in production.

Chapter 9: Industry Applications of LangGraph.js

LangGraph.js is a versatile framework for building agent-based workflows that can be applied across various industries. By leveraging LangGraph.js, organizations can automate processes, improve decision-making, and build intelligent systems that collaborate seamlessly. This chapter explores how LangGraph.js can be used in **E-Commerce**, **Financial Services**, and **AI-powered applications** to address complex challenges and improve operational efficiency.

9.1 E-Commerce

E-commerce businesses handle vast amounts of data and transactions daily. LangGraph.js can be used to automate workflows, enhance customer experiences, and optimize business processes. In this section, we will explore how LangGraph.js can be used for **automating inventory management** and building **intelligent recommendation engines**.

9.1.1 Automating Inventory Management

Effective inventory management is critical for e-commerce businesses to ensure that products are in stock and available for customers when needed. LangGraph.js workflows can automate the monitoring of stock levels, track product movements, and trigger restocking orders.

Key Concepts:

- **Stock Level Monitoring:** Automatically track product stock levels and trigger alerts or orders when stock runs low.
- **Restocking Workflow:** Create workflows that automatically place orders for restocking based on sales data and inventory thresholds.

Example: Inventory Management Workflow

1. **Define Agents:** We will create agents that monitor the stock levels, notify if stock is low, and order new stock automatically.

javascript

```javascript
graph.addAgent('StockMonitor', async (context) => {
  const product = context.data.product;
  const stockLevel = context.data.stockLevel;

  if (stockLevel < 10) {
    console.log(`Low stock alert for ${product}. Placing order for restocking.`);
    context.data.restockOrder = { product, quantity: 100 };
    context.next();
  } else {
    console.log(`${product} has enough stock.`);
    context.next();
  }
});

graph.addAgent('OrderRestock', async (context) => {
  const order = context.data.restockOrder;
  console.log(`Order placed: ${order.product}, Quantity: ${order.quantity}`);
  context.next();
});

graph.defineWorkflow('inventoryWorkflow', ['StockMonitor', 'OrderRestock']);
graph.run('inventoryWorkflow', { product: 'Laptop', stockLevel: 5 });
```

Explanation:

- **Stock Monitoring:** The StockMonitor agent checks the stock level and determines if it is below the restocking threshold (in this case, 10).
- **Restocking Order:** If the stock is low, the OrderRestock agent automatically places an order to restock 100 units.

Best Practices for Inventory Management Workflows:

- **Real-Time Monitoring:** Use real-time data to update stock levels dynamically and trigger automated actions.
- **Threshold Management:** Adjust thresholds for stock levels based on seasonal sales patterns or past data.

9.1.2 Building Intelligent Recommendation Engines

Recommendation engines are a fundamental part of e-commerce websites, helping to drive sales by suggesting products that users are likely to buy. LangGraph.js can be used to build workflows that process user preferences, past behavior, and real-time interactions to deliver personalized recommendations.

Key Concepts:

- **Collaborative Filtering:** Using past user interactions to recommend products similar to those other users have liked.
- **Content-Based Filtering:** Recommending products based on the similarity to items the user has shown interest in.
- **Hybrid Systems:** Combining collaborative and content-based filtering for better recommendations.

Example: Building a Simple Recommendation Engine

javascript

```
graph.addAgent('UserPreferenceAgent', async (context) => {
  const user = context.data.user;
  const purchasedItems = await getUserPurchaseHistory(user);
  const recommendations = await getProductRecommendations(purchasedItems);
```

```
  context.data.recommendations = recommendations;
  context.next();
});

graph.addAgent('RecommendationDisplayAgent', async (context) => {
  const recommendations = context.data.recommendations;
  console.log(`Recommended products for the user: ${recommendations.join(', ')}`);
  context.next();
});

graph.defineWorkflow('recommendationWorkflow', ['UserPreferenceAgent', 'RecommendationDisplayAgent']);
graph.run('recommendationWorkflow', { user: 'user123' });
```

Explanation:

- **User Preferences:** The UserPreferenceAgent fetches the user's purchase history and generates product recommendations.
- **Display Recommendations:** The RecommendationDisplayAgent shows the recommended products to the user.

Best Practices for Building Recommendation Engines:

- **Personalization:** Use user-specific data to offer personalized recommendations.
- **A/B Testing:** Continuously test and refine recommendation algorithms using real-time feedback and A/B testing.

9.2 Financial Services

LangGraph.js is particularly useful in the financial services industry, where workflows need to be highly automated, accurate, and real-time. In this section, we will look at **fraud detection systems** and **real-time transaction monitoring** as key use cases for LangGraph.js.

9.2.1 Fraud Detection Systems

Fraud detection is crucial for preventing financial crimes such as money laundering or unauthorized transactions. LangGraph.js can automate the detection of suspicious patterns in transactions by integrating machine learning models and rule-based systems into workflows.

Key Concepts:

- **Anomaly Detection:** Identifying unusual patterns in transaction data that may indicate fraudulent activity.
- **Rule-Based Systems:** Defining rules that flag specific transactions as suspicious (e.g., large withdrawals, rapid transfers).
- **Machine Learning:** Integrating ML models to classify transactions as legitimate or fraudulent.

Example: Fraud Detection Workflow

javascript

```javascript
graph.addAgent('TransactionValidator', async (context) => {
  const transaction = context.data.transaction;

  if (transaction.amount > 10000) {
    context.data.suspicious = true;
    console.log('Large transaction detected, flagging as suspicious.');
    context.next();
  } else {
    console.log('Transaction amount is within normal limits.');
```

```
    context.next();
  }
});

graph.addAgent('FraudDetectionAgent', async (context) => {
  if (context.data.suspicious) {
    console.log('Transaction flagged for further review.');
  } else {
    console.log('Transaction passed validation.');
  }
  context.next();
});

graph.defineWorkflow('fraudDetectionWorkflow',
['TransactionValidator', 'FraudDetectionAgent']);
graph.run('fraudDetectionWorkflow', { transaction: { amount:
15000, type: 'transfer' } });
```

Explanation:

- **Transaction Validation:** The TransactionValidator agent flags transactions with amounts greater than 10,000 as suspicious.
- **Fraud Detection:** The FraudDetectionAgent reviews flagged transactions and logs them for further investigation.

Best Practices for Fraud Detection Systems:

- **Real-Time Monitoring:** Process transactions in real time to detect fraud as soon as it occurs.
- **Combine Rules with ML:** Use both rule-based and machine learning-based detection methods for more accurate fraud identification.

9.2.2 Real-Time Transaction Monitoring

In financial services, real-time transaction monitoring is essential for detecting and preventing fraud, money laundering, and other illicit activities as they happen. LangGraph.js can process and analyze financial transactions as they occur to identify patterns and anomalies in real time.

Key Concepts:

- **Real-Time Processing:** Continuously monitor and analyze transactions as they are processed.
- **Event-Driven Workflow:** Use events to trigger immediate actions when suspicious activity is detected.

Example: Real-Time Monitoring Workflow

javascript

```
graph.addAgent('RealTimeMonitor', async (context) => {
  const transaction = context.data.transaction;
  if (transaction.type === 'wire_transfer' && transaction.amount > 5000) {
    console.log('High-value wire transfer detected, monitoring closely.');
  }
  context.next();
});

graph.addAgent('MonitorTransaction', async (context) => {
  const transaction = context.data.transaction;
  console.log('Monitoring transaction:', transaction);
  context.next();
});

graph.defineWorkflow('realTimeMonitoringWorkflow', ['RealTimeMonitor', 'MonitorTransaction']);
```

```
graph.run('realTimeMonitoringWorkflow', { transaction: {
type: 'wire_transfer', amount: 6000 } });
```

Explanation:

- **Real-Time Transaction Monitoring:** The RealTimeMonitor agent flags high-value wire transfers and initiates additional monitoring for such transactions.

- **Workflow Execution:** The workflow runs continuously in real time, processing transactions as they come in.

Best Practices for Transaction Monitoring:

- **Immediate Action:** When suspicious behavior is detected, take immediate action such as freezing transactions or alerting security personnel.

- **Machine Learning:** Consider using ML algorithms to continuously improve detection capabilities by learning from past data.

9.3 AI-Powered Applications

LangGraph.js can be used to build sophisticated AI-powered applications that require intelligent workflows, multi-agent collaboration, and real-time data processing. In this section, we will explore **natural language processing (NLP) workflows** and **multi-agent collaboration** for complex tasks.

9.3.1 Natural Language Processing Workflows

Natural language processing is a branch of AI that deals with the interaction between computers and human language. LangGraph.js can be used to build workflows that process and analyze text data, such as chatbot interactions, sentiment analysis, and text classification.

Key Concepts:

- **Text Preprocessing:** Cleaning and formatting raw text data for further analysis.

- **NLP Models:** Use pre-trained NLP models for tasks like sentiment analysis, entity recognition, and text generation.
- **Workflow Automation:** Automate the process of analyzing and responding to user inputs based on NLP results.

Example: NLP Workflow for Sentiment Analysis

javascript

```
const sentiment = require('sentiment');  // Install sentiment package for text analysis

graph.addAgent('TextAnalysisAgent', async (context) => {
  const text = context.data.text;
  const result = sentiment(text);  // Analyze the sentiment of the text
  context.data.sentiment = result.score;  // Store the sentiment score
  context.next();
});

graph.addAgent('SentimentResponseAgent', async (context) => {
  const sentimentScore = context.data.sentiment;
  if (sentimentScore > 0) {
    console.log('Positive sentiment detected.');
  } else if (sentimentScore < 0) {
    console.log('Negative sentiment detected.');
  } else {
    console.log('Neutral sentiment detected.');
  }
  context.next();
});
```

```
graph.defineWorkflow('nlpWorkflow', ['TextAnalysisAgent',
'SentimentResponseAgent']);
graph.run('nlpWorkflow', { text: 'I love using LangGraph.js
for my projects!' });
```

Explanation:

- **Text Analysis:** The TextAnalysisAgent uses the sentiment package to analyze the sentiment of a given text.

- **Response Based on Sentiment:** The SentimentResponseAgent checks the sentiment score and responds accordingly.

Best Practices for NLP Workflows:

- **Text Preprocessing:** Clean and normalize the text (e.g., removing stop words, tokenization) before passing it to NLP models.

- **Use Pre-Trained Models:** Leverage pre-trained models like BERT or GPT-3 for more advanced NLP tasks.

9.3.2 Multi-Agent Collaboration for Complex Tasks

Complex AI tasks often require the collaboration of multiple agents. LangGraph.js makes it easy to coordinate the execution of several agents that work together towards a common goal. This is especially useful for applications such as automated decision-making, recommendation systems, or collaborative problem-solving.

Key Concepts:

- **Multi-Agent Coordination:** Agents collaborate to achieve a shared objective.

- **Task Decomposition:** Break down complex tasks into smaller subtasks that can be handled by different agents.

- **State Sharing:** Agents can share state information to coordinate their efforts.

Example: Multi-Agent Workflow for Task Completion

javascript

```javascript
graph.addAgent('Task1Agent', async (context) => {
  console.log('Starting Task 1');
  context.data.task1Result = 'Task 1 completed';
  context.next();
});

graph.addAgent('Task2Agent', async (context) => {
  console.log('Starting Task 2');
  context.data.task2Result = 'Task 2 completed';
  context.next();
});

graph.addAgent('FinalizerAgent', async (context) => {
  const task1 = context.data.task1Result;
  const task2 = context.data.task2Result;
  console.log(`Finalizing: ${task1}, ${task2}`);
  context.next();
});

graph.defineWorkflow('multiAgentCollaborationWorkflow',
['Task1Agent', 'Task2Agent', 'FinalizerAgent']);
graph.run('multiAgentCollaborationWorkflow');
```

Explanation:

- **Task Decomposition:** The workflow breaks down a complex task into multiple simpler tasks (Task1Agent and Task2Agent).

- **Collaboration:** The agents collaborate by passing results to each other, and the final task is completed by the FinalizerAgent.

Best Practices for Multi-Agent Collaboration:

- **Decouple Tasks:** Ensure that tasks are decoupled so that agents can operate independently as much as possible.
- **State Sharing:** Use shared contexts or message passing to allow agents to communicate and share results.

Summary

In **Chapter 9**, we explored several industry applications of LangGraph.js, including **E-Commerce**, **Financial Services**, and **AI-powered applications**. We saw how LangGraph.js can be used to automate inventory management, build intelligent recommendation engines, detect fraud in financial transactions, and process natural language. By leveraging multi-agent collaboration, you can solve complex tasks that require distributed decision-making and action.

Key Takeaways:

- **E-Commerce:** Use LangGraph.js to automate inventory management and build personalized recommendation engines.
- **Financial Services:** Implement fraud detection systems and real-time transaction monitoring using LangGraph.js workflows.
- **AI-Powered Applications:** Build sophisticated NLP workflows and multi-agent collaboration systems for complex AI tasks.

Chapter 10: Exploring Creative Applications of LangGraph.js

LangGraph.js is a powerful framework for creating agent-based workflows, but its potential extends beyond typical business applications. This chapter explores creative uses of LangGraph.js in **art and music**, **gaming and simulations**, and **experimental multi-agent workflows**. By combining creativity with agent-based design, LangGraph.js can be used to generate art, compose music, design intelligent characters, and even simulate complex environments. Whether you're a developer, artist, or gamer, this chapter will show how LangGraph.js can be applied to a wide range of creative fields.

10.1 Art and Music

LangGraph.js offers unique capabilities for automating creative processes. In the realms of **art** and **music**, agents can be used to generate designs, compositions, and more. This section explores how LangGraph.js can be utilized to create generative art and automate music composition using workflows.

10.1.1 Generative Art with Multi-Agent Systems

Generative art is an artistic practice where algorithms or systems are used to create visuals, often with minimal human intervention. In this case, multi-agent systems in LangGraph.js can be employed to create dynamic art pieces that evolve over time or according to certain rules.

Key Concepts:

- **Algorithmic Art:** The use of algorithms to generate visual art.

- **Collaborative Agents:** Multiple agents can collaborate, each performing a part of the creative process.

- **Randomness and Structure:** Use randomization and rules to create interesting, unpredictable results.

Example: Generative Art with LangGraph.js

1. **Create Agents for Drawing:** We will create agents that draw lines, change colors, and perform random movements to create a piece of art.

javascript

```javascript
graph.addAgent('RandomLineDrawer', async (context) => {
  const canvas = context.data.canvas;
  const startX = Math.random() * canvas.width;
  const startY = Math.random() * canvas.height;
  const endX = Math.random() * canvas.width;
  const endY = Math.random() * canvas.height;

  const color = `rgb(${Math.floor(Math.random() * 255)}, ${Math.floor(Math.random() * 255)}, ${Math.floor(Math.random() * 255)})`;
  canvas.drawLine(startX, startY, endX, endY, color); // Custom method for drawing lines on a canvas
  context.next();
});

graph.addAgent('RandomColorChanger', async (context) => {
  const canvas = context.data.canvas;
  const color = `rgb(${Math.floor(Math.random() * 255)}, ${Math.floor(Math.random() * 255)}, ${Math.floor(Math.random() * 255)})`;
  canvas.changeBackgroundColor(color); // Custom method for changing background color
  context.next();
});
```

```
graph.defineWorkflow('generativeArtWorkflow',
['RandomLineDrawer', 'RandomColorChanger']);
graph.run('generativeArtWorkflow', { canvas: new Canvas(500,
500) }); // Assume a Canvas class that handles drawing
```

Explanation:

- **Random Line Drawing:** The RandomLineDrawer agent randomly generates lines with random starting and ending points, creating an evolving piece of art.

- **Color Changing:** The RandomColorChanger agent changes the background color after every few iterations, adding more complexity to the artwork.

- **Canvas Object:** A Canvas object is used to simulate drawing, and you can replace it with actual canvas drawing logic if you're using an HTML5 <canvas> element or any other graphic environment.

Best Practices for Generative Art Workflows:

- **Agent Collaboration:** Use multiple agents working together, each contributing a different aspect of the artwork (e.g., drawing, coloring, positioning).

- **Controlled Randomness:** While randomness plays a key role in generative art, you can introduce constraints or patterns to guide the output while maintaining an element of unpredictability.

10.1.2 Music Composition Using Agent Workflows

LangGraph.js can be used to automate music composition by designing workflows where agents generate musical notes, rhythms, and melodies. These agents can be coordinated to create dynamic and evolving compositions that follow certain patterns or are entirely random.

Key Concepts:

- **Generative Music:** Creating music algorithmically, often with minimal human input.

- **Harmonic and Rhythmic Agents:** Agents can focus on specific aspects of music, such as harmony, rhythm, or melody.
- **Real-Time Music Generation:** Music can be generated in real time, adapting to user input or changing conditions.

Example: Music Composition Workflow

1. **Define Music Agents:** We will create agents that generate random notes and rhythms.

javascript

```javascript
const musicGenerator = require('music-generator'); // Assume a music generation library

graph.addAgent('RhythmAgent', async (context) => {
  const rhythmPattern = ['quarter', 'eighth', 'dottedQuarter', 'whole']; // Define rhythm patterns
  const rhythm = rhythmPattern[Math.floor(Math.random() * rhythmPattern.length)];
  context.data.rhythm = rhythm;
  console.log('Rhythm:', rhythm);
  context.next();
});

graph.addAgent('MelodyAgent', async (context) => {
  const melody = musicGenerator.generateMelody(); // Using a music generation library to generate a melody
  context.data.melody = melody;
  console.log('Melody:', melody);
  context.next();
});

graph.addAgent('ComposerAgent', async (context) => {
```

```
  const rhythm = context.data.rhythm;
  const melody = context.data.melody;
  console.log(`Composition: Rhythm - ${rhythm}, Melody - ${melody}`);
  context.next();
});

graph.defineWorkflow('musicCompositionWorkflow', ['RhythmAgent', 'MelodyAgent', 'ComposerAgent']);
graph.run('musicCompositionWorkflow');
```

Explanation:

- **Rhythm and Melody Agents:** The RhythmAgent generates random rhythmic patterns, and the MelodyAgent generates a melody using a predefined music generation library.

- **Composition:** The ComposerAgent combines both the melody and rhythm to produce a full composition.

Best Practices for Music Composition Workflows:

- **Modular Agents:** Define distinct agents for different components of music, such as melody, rhythm, harmony, and dynamics.

- **Feedback Loops:** Allow the workflow to evolve iteratively, with agents modifying the music based on past outputs (e.g., adjusting melody based on rhythm).

10.2 Gaming and Simulations

LangGraph.js can also be used in **gaming** and **simulation** environments, where intelligent non-player characters (NPCs) and complex environments need to be modeled. This section will explore how to design intelligent NPCs and simulate complex environments using multi-agent workflows.

10.2.1 Designing Intelligent NPCs

In games, **NPCs** (non-player characters) are responsible for interacting with players and carrying out predefined actions. LangGraph.js can be used to create workflows for intelligent NPCs that adapt to the player's behavior and the game's environment.

Key Concepts:

- **Reactive NPCs:** NPCs that respond to player actions in real-time.
- **Proactive NPCs:** NPCs that plan their actions based on game goals, such as completing quests or defending an area.
- **Behavior Trees:** Organize NPC behaviors into trees that can be evaluated at runtime.

Example: NPC Behavior Workflow

javascript

```javascript
graph.addAgent('PatrolAgent', async (context) => {
  const npc = context.data.npc;
  npc.patrolArea();
  console.log(`${npc.name} is patrolling the area.`);
  context.next();
});

graph.addAgent('AttackAgent', async (context) => {
  const npc = context.data.npc;
  if (npc.detectPlayer()) {
    npc.attackPlayer();
    console.log(`${npc.name} is attacking the player.`);
  }
  context.next();
});
```

```
graph.defineWorkflow('npcBehaviorWorkflow', ['PatrolAgent',
'AttackAgent']);
graph.run('npcBehaviorWorkflow', { npc: new NPC('Guard',
'patrol') });
```

Explanation:

- **Patrol and Attack Behaviors:** The PatrolAgent makes the NPC patrol an area, while the AttackAgent triggers an attack if the NPC detects a player in the vicinity.
- **NPC Context:** The npc object is passed through the context, allowing the agents to share and update the NPC's state.

Best Practices for NPC Design:

- **Modular Behaviors:** Break down NPC behaviors into smaller, reusable agents that can be combined in different ways.
- **State Management:** Use the context object to manage NPC state, such as health, position, and objectives.

10.2.2 Simulating Complex Environments

LangGraph.js can also be used to simulate complex environments where multiple entities interact with each other. These simulations can model physical systems, economic models, or even social dynamics.

Key Concepts:

- **Multi-Agent Environments:** Multiple agents working in parallel, interacting with each other and their environment.
- **Simulation Steps:** Each step in the simulation represents an interaction or update in the environment.

Example: Simulating a Traffic System

javascript

```
graph.addAgent('CarAgent', async (context) => {
```

```
  const car = context.data.car;
  car.move();  // Simulate car movement
  console.log(`Car ${car.id} is moving.`);
  context.next();
});

graph.addAgent('TrafficLightAgent', async (context) => {
  const light = context.data.trafficLight;
  light.toggle();  // Simulate traffic light change
  console.log(`Traffic light is now ${light.status}`);
  context.next();
});

graph.defineWorkflow('trafficSimulationWorkflow',
['CarAgent', 'TrafficLightAgent']);
graph.run('trafficSimulationWorkflow', {
  car: new Car(1),
  trafficLight: new TrafficLight('green'),
});
```

Explanation:

- **Car and Traffic Light Agents:** The CarAgent simulates a car's movement, while the TrafficLightAgent simulates the changing of a traffic light.

- **Interaction:** The two agents interact in the workflow, representing a basic traffic simulation.

Best Practices for Simulation Workflows:

- **Stepwise Simulation:** Break down the simulation into discrete steps, with each agent performing a specific action.

- **Realistic Interactions:** Ensure that agent interactions are modeled realistically, reflecting the dynamics of the system you're simulating.

10.3 Experimental Multi-Agent Workflows

LangGraph.js offers incredible flexibility for experimenting with new use cases. In this section, we explore innovative applications and how to push the boundaries of what LangGraph.js can achieve.

10.3.1 Innovative Use Cases

LangGraph.js can be applied to fields beyond traditional use cases, such as **automated research** in scientific fields, **creative writing**, or even **robotics**. The flexibility of the agent-based design allows LangGraph.js to be adapted to virtually any problem that involves autonomous decision-making and coordination.

Key Concepts:

- **Autonomous Research:** Agents can autonomously collect, analyze, and synthesize data for scientific research or problem-solving.
- **Creative Writing:** Agents can collaborate to generate story plots, dialogue, or even entire books.

Example: Autonomous Scientific Research Workflow

javascript

```javascript
graph.addAgent('DataCollectorAgent', async (context) => {
  const data = await fetchScientificData();
  context.data.researchData = data;
  context.next();
});

graph.addAgent('DataAnalyzerAgent', async (context) => {
  const analysisResults = analyzeData(context.data.researchData);
  context.data.analysis = analysisResults;
  context.next();
```

```
});

graph.defineWorkflow('scientificResearchWorkflow',
['DataCollectorAgent', 'DataAnalyzerAgent']);
graph.run('scientificResearchWorkflow');
```

Explanation:

- **Data Collection and Analysis:** The DataCollectorAgent gathers research data, and the DataAnalyzerAgent processes and analyzes it, demonstrating how LangGraph.js can automate research tasks.

10.3.2 Pushing the Boundaries of LangGraph.js

LangGraph.js's flexibility allows developers to experiment with innovative ideas that go beyond traditional applications. By integrating LangGraph.js with other technologies (e.g., machine learning models, IoT devices, or cloud computing), you can create even more powerful workflows.

Key Concepts:

- **Cross-Technology Integration:** Combine LangGraph.js with other tools and technologies to create hybrid systems.
- **Exploring New Domains:** LangGraph.js can be applied to fields like **artificial life**, **swarm robotics**, or even **interactive performance art**.

Example: Integrating LangGraph.js with IoT Devices for Smart Home Automation

javascript

```javascript
graph.addAgent('TemperatureSensorAgent', async (context) => {
  const temperature = await readTemperatureFromSensor(); // Simulate reading from IoT device
  context.data.temperature = temperature;
  context.next();
```

```
});

graph.addAgent('SmartThermostatAgent', async (context) => {
  const temperature = context.data.temperature;
  if (temperature > 75) {
    console.log('Temperature is too high, turning on the AC.');
  } else {
    console.log('Temperature is comfortable, no action needed.');
  }
  context.next();
});

graph.defineWorkflow('smartHomeWorkflow', ['TemperatureSensorAgent', 'SmartThermostatAgent']);
graph.run('smartHomeWorkflow');
```

Explanation:

- **IoT Integration:** This workflow integrates LangGraph.js with an IoT temperature sensor and a smart thermostat agent to create a basic smart home automation system.

Summary

In **Chapter 10**, we explored creative applications of LangGraph.js in art, music, gaming, simulations, and experimental workflows. LangGraph.js's flexibility allows it to be applied in a wide range of creative fields, from generating art and composing music to designing intelligent NPCs and simulating complex environments. By using multi-agent systems, developers can automate complex tasks, generate creative content, and push the boundaries of what can be achieved with agent-based workflows.

Key Takeaways:

- **Generative Art and Music:** LangGraph.js can be used to create dynamic, evolving art and music compositions with multiple agents working together.

- **Gaming and Simulations:** Design intelligent NPCs and simulate complex environments with multi-agent systems.

- **Innovative Use Cases:** LangGraph.js can be adapted to a wide range of experimental applications, from autonomous scientific research to smart home automation.

Chapter 11: Hands-On Projects

In this chapter, we'll dive into practical, real-world applications of LangGraph.js through hands-on projects. These projects will allow you to apply the concepts you've learned so far to build real-time, intelligent systems. We will walk you through building a **real-time chat application**, a **multi-agent IoT monitoring system**, and an **e-commerce recommendation system**. These projects will help you understand how to implement LangGraph.js in various use cases and scale your applications effectively.

11.1 Real-Time Chat Application

Chat applications are a popular use case for real-time systems. By integrating LangGraph.js, you can create intelligent chatbots that can respond to user messages, interact with external services, and perform tasks like scheduling or information retrieval. In this section, we will walk through building a **chatbot** using LangGraph.js and integrating it with WebSockets and frontend frameworks for real-time interaction.

11.1.1 Building a Chatbot Using LangGraph.js

A **chatbot** can be built by creating a series of agents that interpret user inputs, respond accordingly, and perform actions. LangGraph.js allows you to orchestrate these agents into a workflow, ensuring that the chatbot behaves intelligently and responsively.

Key Concepts:

- **Chatbot Workflow:** Sequence of agents that handle user input, process it, and return a response.

- **Intent Recognition:** Detecting the user's intent from the message and deciding what action to take.

- **Context Management:** Maintaining context across interactions, such as remembering the user's previous messages or responses.

Example: Simple Chatbot Workflow

Let's build a simple chatbot that can respond to greetings and provide information about the weather.

1. **Define Agents:**

javascript

```javascript
graph.addAgent('GreetingAgent', async (context) => {
  const message = context.data.message;
  if (message.toLowerCase().includes('hello')) {
    context.data.response = 'Hello! How can I assist you today?';
  } else {
    context.next();
  }
});

graph.addAgent('WeatherAgent', async (context) => {
  const message = context.data.message;
  if (message.toLowerCase().includes('weather')) {
    // Fetching weather information (mocked for simplicity)
    context.data.response = 'The weather is sunny and 25° C today!';
  } else {
    context.next();
  }
});

graph.addAgent('DefaultAgent', async (context) => {
  context.data.response = 'Sorry, I didn't understand that. Can you ask something else?';
```

```
  context.next();
});
```

```
graph.defineWorkflow('chatbotWorkflow', ['GreetingAgent',
'WeatherAgent', 'DefaultAgent']);
```

Explanation:

- **GreetingAgent:** This agent checks if the message contains the word "hello" and responds accordingly.
- **WeatherAgent:** If the message includes "weather," it responds with a hardcoded weather message.
- **DefaultAgent:** If none of the above agents respond, this agent provides a default response indicating that the bot didn't understand the input.

2. **Running the Chatbot Workflow:**

javascript

```javascript
const userMessage = 'What is the weather today?';
graph.run('chatbotWorkflow', { message: userMessage }, (context) => {
  console.log(context.data.response); // Output: 'The weather is sunny and 25° C today!'
});
```

Best Practices for Chatbot Development:

- **Intent Detection:** Use simple keyword matching or integrate natural language processing (NLP) models to better understand user queries.
- **Context Management:** Store user preferences or session data to personalize interactions.
- **Error Handling:** Ensure that your chatbot gracefully handles unrecognized inputs and provides fallback responses.

11.1.2 Integrating with WebSocket and Frontend Frameworks

WebSockets are an essential part of real-time applications like chatbots, as they allow full-duplex communication channels between the server and the client. By integrating LangGraph.js with WebSockets and a frontend framework like React.js, you can build a highly responsive chat application.

Key Concepts:

- **WebSocket Communication:** Allows real-time, bidirectional communication between the server and the client.
- **React.js Integration:** React's state management and component-based structure work well for handling dynamic updates in a chat interface.

Example: Integrating LangGraph.js with WebSocket

1. **Setting Up WebSocket Server:**

javascript

```javascript
const WebSocket = require('ws');
const wsServer = new WebSocket.Server({ port: 8080 });

wsServer.on('connection', (ws) => {
  ws.on('message', async (message) => {
    console.log('Received:', message);

    // Run LangGraph.js workflow based on received message
    await graph.run('chatbotWorkflow', { message: message }, (context) => {
      ws.send(context.data.response); // Send the response back to the client
    });
  });
});
```

});

2. **React.js Frontend Integration:**

Here's how you can integrate the WebSocket server with a React.js frontend to create a real-time chat interface.

javascript

```
import React, { useState, useEffect } from 'react';

const Chatbot = () => {
  const [messages, setMessages] = useState([]);
  const [input, setInput] = useState('');
  const [socket, setSocket] = useState(null);

  useEffect(() => {
    const ws = new WebSocket('ws://localhost:8080');
    ws.onopen = () => console.log('Connected to WebSocket server');
    ws.onmessage = (event) => {
      const newMessage = event.data;
      setMessages((prevMessages) => [...prevMessages, newMessage]);
    };
    setSocket(ws);
  }, []);

  const sendMessage = () => {
    if (socket) {
      socket.send(input);
      setMessages((prevMessages) => [...prevMessages, `You: ${input}`]);
```

```
      setInput('');
    }
  };

  return (
    <div>
      <div className="chat-window">
        {messages.map((message, index) => (
          <div key={index}>{message}</div>
        ))}
      </div>
      <input
        type="text"
        value={input}
        onChange={(e) => setInput(e.target.value)}
        placeholder="Type a message..."
      />
      <button onClick={sendMessage}>Send</button>
    </div>
  );
};

export default Chatbot;
```

Explanation:

- **WebSocket Client (React.js):** The React app connects to the WebSocket server and sends user input. It listens for messages from the server and updates the chat interface in real-time.

- **LangGraph.js Workflow (Server-side):** When the WebSocket server receives a message, it triggers the LangGraph.js workflow to process the message and send a response back to the client.

Best Practices for Real-Time Applications:

- **Efficient State Management:** Use frameworks like React or Redux to handle application state and ensure the UI updates efficiently.

- **Connection Management:** Ensure that WebSocket connections are properly managed and closed to avoid memory leaks.

- **User Experience:** Provide real-time feedback, such as typing indicators, to improve user engagement.

11.2 IoT Monitoring Workflow

IoT (Internet of Things) systems often involve multiple devices collecting and transmitting data in real time. LangGraph.js can be used to create workflows that process IoT data, trigger alerts, and analyze sensor readings. In this section, we will design an **agent-based IoT system** and use LangGraph.js to handle data processing and alerts.

11.2.1 Designing Agent-Based IoT Systems

In an IoT system, sensors gather data (e.g., temperature, humidity, or pressure) that needs to be processed. LangGraph.js can be used to create workflows that monitor these devices, process their data, and trigger actions based on certain conditions (e.g., alerting when a threshold is exceeded).

Key Concepts:

- **Sensor Agents:** These agents simulate the collection of data from IoT devices.

- **Alert Agents:** Trigger alerts when sensor readings exceed predefined thresholds.

- **Data Aggregation:** Combine data from multiple sensors to provide a comprehensive view of the environment.

Example: IoT Monitoring Workflow

1. **Create Agent for Data Collection:**

javascript

```javascript
graph.addAgent('SensorAgent', async (context) => {
  const temperature = await getTemperatureSensorData(); // Simulate reading from a temperature sensor
  context.data.temperature = temperature;
  context.next();
});
```

2. **Create Agent for Alerting:**

javascript

```javascript
graph.addAgent('AlertAgent', async (context) => {
  const temperature = context.data.temperature;
  if (temperature > 30) {
    context.data.alert = 'Temperature is too high! Triggering alarm.';
  } else {
    context.data.alert = 'Temperature is normal.';
  }
  context.next();
});
```

3. **Run the Workflow:**

javascript

```javascript
graph.defineWorkflow('iotMonitoringWorkflow', ['SensorAgent', 'AlertAgent']);
graph.run('iotMonitoringWorkflow');
```

Explanation:

- **Sensor Agent:** The SensorAgent collects temperature data from a simulated IoT device.

- **Alert Agent:** The AlertAgent checks if the temperature exceeds a threshold (30°C) and triggers an alert if necessary.

Best Practices for IoT Systems:

- **Data Filtering:** Filter and preprocess raw data from sensors before further analysis to remove noise or irrelevant data.
- **Real-Time Processing:** Process data in real-time to trigger timely alerts and actions.
- **Efficient Data Storage:** Use efficient data storage solutions for large volumes of data generated by IoT devices.

11.2.2 Using LangGraph.js for Data Processing and Alerts

LangGraph.js can process sensor data, trigger alerts, and even integrate with external systems like email or SMS services for notifications.

Example: Sending an Alert via Email

javascript

```javascript
graph.addAgent('EmailAlertAgent', async (context) => {
  const alertMessage = context.data.alert;
  if (alertMessage) {
    await sendEmailAlert(alertMessage); // Send an email notification
    console.log('Alert email sent:', alertMessage);
  }
  context.next();
});
```

Explanation:

- **Email Alerting:** The EmailAlertAgent sends an email when an alert is triggered, using a third-party service like **Nodemailer** or **SendGrid**.

11.3 E-Commerce Recommendation System

Recommendation systems are key to driving sales in e-commerce platforms by suggesting products to users based on their browsing history, purchases, and preferences. In this section, we will build a **multi-agent recommendation engine** using LangGraph.js and discuss how to **scale** it for large datasets.

11.3.1 Building a Multi-Agent Recommendation Engine

A recommendation engine typically relies on collaborative filtering (user-based or item-based) and content-based filtering. We will create a multi-agent system where agents process user data, match items, and generate personalized recommendations.

Key Concepts:

- **Collaborative Filtering:** Recommend products based on the preferences of similar users.
- **Content-Based Filtering:** Recommend products based on the features of the products the user has shown interest in.

Example: Building a Simple Recommendation Engine

1. **Define User Agent:**

javascript

```
graph.addAgent('UserAgent', async (context) => {
  const userPreferences = await getUserPreferences(context.data.userId);
  context.data.userPreferences = userPreferences;
  context.next();
});
```

2. **Define Item Matching Agent:**

javascript

```
graph.addAgent('ItemMatchingAgent', async (context) => {
```

```javascript
  const preferences = context.data.userPreferences;
  const recommendedItems = await
recommendItemsBasedOnPreferences(preferences);
  context.data.recommendedItems = recommendedItems;
  context.next();
});
```

3. **Display Recommendations:**

javascript

```javascript
graph.addAgent('DisplayRecommendations', async (context) => {
  const recommendedItems = context.data.recommendedItems;
  console.log('Recommended items for the user:', recommendedItems);
  context.next();
});

graph.defineWorkflow('recommendationEngineWorkflow',
['UserAgent', 'ItemMatchingAgent',
'DisplayRecommendations']);
```

Explanation:

- **User Preferences:** The UserAgent fetches the user's preferences based on past interactions.
- **Item Matching:** The ItemMatchingAgent matches items based on these preferences and generates recommendations.
- **Display Recommendations:** The DisplayRecommendations agent shows the recommended items to the user.

11.3.2 Scaling for Large Datasets

As your e-commerce platform grows, so does the amount of data. You need to ensure that your recommendation system can scale to handle large numbers of users and products.

Key Concepts:

- **Distributed Data Processing:** Use distributed systems to process large datasets in parallel.

- **Caching Recommendations:** Cache frequently requested recommendations to reduce load and speed up response times.

Best Practices for Scaling Recommendation Systems:

- **Use Parallel Processing:** Break down the recommendation tasks into smaller, parallelizable jobs (e.g., recommending items in batches).

- **Implement Caching:** Cache recommendation results to quickly serve popular products without recalculating them each time.

Summary

In **Chapter 11**, we explored hands-on projects that demonstrate how to implement LangGraph.js in real-world applications. We covered building a **real-time chat application**, a **multi-agent IoT monitoring system**, and an **e-commerce recommendation system**. These projects helped showcase LangGraph.js's versatility in creating dynamic workflows, integrating with external systems, and scaling applications effectively.

Key Takeaways:

- **Chat Applications:** Use LangGraph.js to build intelligent chatbots with WebSocket integration.

- **IoT Systems:** Monitor and process IoT data, trigger alerts, and create real-time workflows.

- **Recommendation Engines:** Build personalized recommendation systems and scale them for large datasets.

Chapter 12: Extending LangGraph.js

LangGraph.js is a flexible and powerful framework for creating agent-based workflows. However, its full potential can be realized when you extend it and contribute to the broader LangGraph.js ecosystem. In this chapter, we will cover how to **contribute** to LangGraph.js, **integrate it with other libraries** for enhanced functionality, and **build a thriving LangGraph.js ecosystem** through collaboration and community-driven projects.

12.1 Contributing to LangGraph.js

As an open-source framework, LangGraph.js thrives on community contributions. Whether you're interested in improving the core functionality, adding plugins, or helping with documentation, your contributions can have a significant impact on the project. This section will guide you on how to get involved in the LangGraph.js open-source ecosystem and how to write and submit plugins.

12.1.1 Understanding the Open Source Ecosystem

LangGraph.js is part of a large open-source community where developers, contributors, and users collaborate to improve and extend the project. Open-source contributions are crucial for the growth of the project, allowing it to evolve based on the needs of the community.

Key Concepts:

- **Forking and Cloning:** To contribute to LangGraph.js, you will typically fork the repository, make changes, and then submit a pull request.

- **Issue Tracking:** Use the issue tracker to report bugs, suggest features, or request help.

- **Version Control:** LangGraph.js uses Git and GitHub for version control, making collaboration easier.

Steps to Contribute:

1. **Fork the Repository:** Start by forking the LangGraph.js repository to your GitHub account.

2. **Clone the Repository:** Clone your forked repository to your local machine for development.

bash

```
git clone https://github.com/yourusername/langgraph.js.git
```

3. **Set Up the Development Environment:** Install all the dependencies and ensure you have the right version of Node.js installed. You can use the following command to install dependencies:

bash

```
npm install
```

4. **Make Changes:** Work on the feature or bug fix you want to contribute. Ensure you follow the coding standards and best practices set by the LangGraph.js team.

5. **Commit Your Changes:** Write clear commit messages that describe the changes you've made. For example:

bash

```
git commit -m "Fixed issue with agent execution order"
```

6. **Submit a Pull Request (PR):** After pushing your changes, submit a pull request to the main repository. The LangGraph.js maintainers will review your changes and provide feedback.

Best Practices for Contributing:

- **Clear Commit Messages:** Be descriptive and concise in your commit messages.
- **Write Tests:** Ensure that you write tests to verify the functionality of your changes.
- **Follow Code Style Guidelines:** Maintain consistency in coding style by following the conventions outlined in the repository.

12.1.2 Writing and Submitting Plugins

LangGraph.js is highly extensible, and one of the best ways to contribute is by writing plugins. Plugins are additional modules or functionalities that extend LangGraph.js, such as new types of agents, additional utilities, or integrations with other libraries.

Key Concepts:

- **Plugins:** Independent modules that extend the core LangGraph.js functionality.
- **Agent Plugins:** Define custom agents that can be added to workflows.
- **Utility Plugins:** Add extra features or utilities, such as data validation, logging, or error handling.

Example: Writing a Plugin for LangGraph.js

Let's say we want to write a plugin that adds a new agent to LangGraph.js. This agent will fetch data from an external API.

1. **Define the Agent Plugin:**

javascript

```javascript
// api-fetcher-agent.js
module.exports = function (graph) {
  graph.addAgent('ApiFetcherAgent', async (context) => {
    const data = await fetchDataFromAPI('https://api.example.com/data');
```

```
    context.data.apiData = data;
    context.next();
  });
};

// Register the agent plugin in LangGraph.js
const apiFetcherPlugin = require('./api-fetcher-agent');
apiFetcherPlugin(graph);
```

Explanation:

- **Agent Definition:** The ApiFetcherAgent is defined to fetch data from an external API and store the response in the context.

- **Plugin Registration:** After defining the agent, the plugin is registered by invoking it in the LangGraph.js instance.

2. **Submit the Plugin:**
    - Once your plugin is working and well-documented, you can submit it by creating a pull request to the LangGraph.js plugin repository or to the main repository if it's a core feature.

Best Practices for Plugin Development:

- **Modularity:** Design your plugins to be self-contained and reusable.

- **Documentation:** Provide clear instructions on how to use your plugin, including installation steps and examples.

- **Testing:** Write tests for your plugin to ensure that it behaves as expected.

12.2 Using LangGraph.js with Other Libraries

One of LangGraph.js's strengths is its ability to integrate with other libraries and technologies. In this section, we will discuss how to use

LangGraph.js with **TensorFlow.js** for AI tasks and **D3.js** for data visualization.

12.2.1 Integrating TensorFlow.js for AI Tasks

TensorFlow.js is a powerful library for machine learning in JavaScript. By integrating TensorFlow.js with LangGraph.js, you can add intelligent decision-making capabilities to your agent workflows.

Key Concepts:

- **Machine Learning Models:** TensorFlow.js can be used to load pre-trained models or train new models for specific tasks.
- **Data Flow Integration:** LangGraph.js workflows can feed data into TensorFlow.js models and use the model's output to influence agent actions.

Example: Using TensorFlow.js with LangGraph.js

Let's create a workflow where an agent uses a pre-trained machine learning model to classify images.

1. **Install TensorFlow.js:**

bash

```
npm install @tensorflow/tfjs
```

2. **Create an Image Classification Agent:**

javascript

```
const tf = require('@tensorflow/tfjs');

graph.addAgent('ImageClassifierAgent', async (context) => {
  const imageData = context.data.image; // Assume image data is passed in the context
  const model = await tf.loadLayersModel('https://model-url/model.json');
```

```
  // Perform image classification
  const predictions = model.predict(tf.tensor(imageData));
  context.data.predictions = predictions.arraySync();
  context.next();
});

graph.run('imageClassificationWorkflow', { image: someImageData });
```

Explanation:

- **TensorFlow.js Integration:** The ImageClassifierAgent uses TensorFlow.js to load a pre-trained model and classify input image data.

- **Model Prediction:** After running the model, the predictions are stored in the workflow's context for further processing.

Best Practices for Using AI Models:

- **Model Optimization:** Ensure that models are optimized for use in JavaScript (e.g., using TensorFlow.js's converter tools).

- **Data Preprocessing:** Preprocess input data to match the format expected by the model.

- **Batch Processing:** For large datasets, consider using batch processing to improve performance.

12.2.2 Combining LangGraph.js with D3.js for Visualization

D3.js is a JavaScript library for creating interactive data visualizations. Integrating D3.js with LangGraph.js allows you to visualize the data processed by your agent workflows, making it easier to analyze and present the results.

Key Concepts:

- **Data Binding:** D3.js binds data to DOM elements and updates the visual representation based on changes in the data.

- **Dynamic Visualizations:** Use LangGraph.js agents to generate or modify data, and D3.js to visualize that data in real time.

Example: Visualizing Agent Data with D3.js

1. **Install D3.js:**

bash

```
npm install d3
```

2. **Create a Data Visualization Agent:**

javascript

```
const d3 = require('d3');

graph.addAgent('DataVisualizationAgent', async (context) => {
  const data = context.data.chartData;  // Assume chart data is passed in the context
  const svg = d3.select('svg');

  // Bind the data to elements and create a bar chart
  const bars = svg.selectAll('rect')
    .data(data)
    .enter().append('rect')
    .attr('x', (d, i) => i * 30)
    .attr('y', d => 100 - d)
    .attr('width', 20)
    .attr('height', d => d);

  context.next();
});
```

```
graph.run('dataVisualizationWorkflow', { chartData: [30, 60, 90, 120, 150] });
```

Explanation:

- **Data Binding:** The DataVisualizationAgent binds the data passed through the workflow to SVG elements, creating a simple bar chart using D3.js.

- **Real-Time Visualization:** As agents update the data, the chart is dynamically updated.

Best Practices for Data Visualization:

- **Interactive Visualizations:** Use D3.js's interactivity features to allow users to explore data through zooming, panning, or hovering.

- **Update in Real Time:** Use LangGraph.js's real-time workflows to update visualizations dynamically as new data comes in.

12.3 Building the LangGraph.js Ecosystem

The LangGraph.js ecosystem is not just about the core framework but also about fostering a community of contributors and collaborators. In this section, we will explore how to build and maintain a thriving ecosystem, focusing on **community contributions** and **collaborative projects**.

12.3.1 Fostering Community Contributions

A thriving open-source ecosystem is driven by active contributions from the community. To foster contributions, it's essential to maintain clear documentation, provide guidelines for contributing, and create an inclusive and welcoming environment.

Key Concepts:

- **Documentation:** Well-maintained documentation helps new contributors understand the project and start contributing quickly.

- **Contribution Guidelines:** Clearly defined guidelines ensure that contributions are consistent and follow best practices.
- **Community Engagement:** Actively engage with the community through forums, chat channels, and social media to encourage contributions.

Best Practices for Fostering Community Contributions:

- **Clear Issues:** Label issues in the GitHub repository as "good first issue" to guide newcomers.
- **Encourage Discussions:** Use platforms like GitHub Discussions or Slack channels to answer questions and discuss new ideas.
- **Maintain Code Quality:** Set standards for code quality, including writing tests and adhering to style guides.

12.3.2 Collaborating on Open-Source Projects

LangGraph.js can be extended and improved by collaborating with other open-source projects. Integrating LangGraph.js with other frameworks or libraries can provide more value to users and attract a larger community.

Key Concepts:

- **Cross-Project Collaboration:** LangGraph.js can integrate with other open-source projects to extend its functionality.
- **Shared Repositories:** Collaborating on repositories with other open-source projects helps in building tools that benefit multiple communities.

Example: Collaborating on a Machine Learning Integration

LangGraph.js could be integrated with popular machine learning libraries like **TensorFlow.js**, **Keras.js**, or **Brain.js** to enhance the workflow system with AI capabilities.

Best Practices for Collaboration:

- **Define Integration Points:** Clearly define how LangGraph.js integrates with other libraries, and document those integration points.

- **Contribute to Other Projects:** Look for opportunities to contribute to other open-source projects that could benefit LangGraph.js, and vice versa.

Summary

In **Chapter 12**, we explored how to extend LangGraph.js by contributing to its open-source ecosystem, integrating it with other libraries, and collaborating with the community. We covered:

- **Contributing to LangGraph.js:** How to fork, clone, and contribute changes, including writing and submitting plugins.

- **Using LangGraph.js with Other Libraries:** How to extend LangGraph.js by integrating it with TensorFlow.js for AI tasks and D3.js for data visualization.

- **Building the Ecosystem:** How to foster community contributions and collaborate on open-source projects to grow the LangGraph.js ecosystem.

Chapter 13: Interactive Learning with LangGraph.js

Interactive learning is one of the most effective ways to grasp complex programming concepts, especially when dealing with a framework like LangGraph.js. This chapter is designed to provide you with a structured approach to engaging with LangGraph.js in a hands-on way. You will learn how to set up interactive coding environments, tackle coding challenges, receive real-time feedback, and even participate in gamified challenges to enhance your understanding of agent workflows.

13.1 Using CodeSandbox or StackBlitz

CodeSandbox and StackBlitz are powerful online integrated development environments (IDEs) that allow you to quickly start coding without the need for extensive setup. Both platforms enable you to create and share projects, making them ideal for learning and collaborating in real-time. In this section, we will guide you through setting up LangGraph.js in these environments, sharing your projects, and collaborating with others.

13.1.1 Setting Up Interactive Coding Environments

Both **CodeSandbox** and **StackBlitz** offer cloud-based IDEs that provide you with an instant coding environment. You can write, test, and share your LangGraph.js projects directly in the browser.

Using CodeSandbox:

1. **Navigate to CodeSandbox:**
    - Visit CodeSandbox and click on **Create Sandbox**.
2. **Choose a Template:**
    - Select **Node.js** or **React** (depending on your project type). This will set up a default project with a file structure suitable for LangGraph.js development.

- If you are working on a backend application, choose the **Node.js** template.

3. **Install LangGraph.js:**
    - Open the **package.json** file and add LangGraph.js as a dependency by entering the following in the dependencies section:

json

```json
{
  "dependencies": {
    "langgraph": "^1.0.0"
  }
}
```

- CodeSandbox automatically installs the dependencies for you, so you can start coding right away.

4. **Start Coding:**
    - Open the **index.js** or **app.js** file and start writing your LangGraph.js code. Example:

javascript

```javascript
import { Graph } from 'langgraph';

const graph = new Graph();

graph.addAgent('GreetingAgent', async (context) => {
  context.data.message = 'Hello from LangGraph.js!';
  context.next();
});

graph.run('greetingWorkflow', {});
```

Using StackBlitz:

1. **Navigate to StackBlitz:**
   - Visit StackBlitz and click on **Create New Project**.

2. **Select a Template:**
   - Choose **Node.js** or **JavaScript** based on your project needs.

3. **Install LangGraph.js:**
   - In the **package.json** file, add LangGraph.js under dependencies:

json

```
{
  "dependencies": {
    "langgraph": "^1.0.0"
  }
}
```

   - StackBlitz will automatically install LangGraph.js, and you can start coding immediately.

4. **Write Your Code:**
   - In the **index.js** or main file, write your LangGraph.js code. Example:

javascript

```
const { Graph } = require('langgraph');
const graph = new Graph();

graph.addAgent('GreetingAgent', async (context) => {
  context.data.message = 'Hello, welcome to LangGraph.js!';
  context.next();
```

```
});

graph.run('greetingWorkflow', {});
```

Best Practices for Interactive Coding Environments:

- **Live Preview:** Both CodeSandbox and StackBlitz provide instant live previews of your code, allowing you to see results in real-time.

- **Environment Customization:** Customize your development environment based on the complexity of your LangGraph.js workflows, such as adding packages or modifying settings.

- **Avoid Overloading:** Keep your code modular, and break down complex workflows into smaller, manageable pieces.

13.1.2 Sharing and Collaborating on Projects

One of the great features of using online IDEs like CodeSandbox and StackBlitz is the ability to share and collaborate on projects in real time. These platforms allow you to share links to your projects, enabling others to see your code, give feedback, or even collaborate on it directly.

How to Share Projects:

1. **In CodeSandbox:**
   - After you've completed a project, click on the **"Share"** button at the top-right corner of the screen.
   - You will get a unique URL that you can share with others. Anyone with the link can access your project and even make edits if you allow it.

2. **In StackBlitz:**
   - Click on the **"Share"** button in the top-right corner.
   - You will receive a link to your project. Share this link with collaborators, or use it to showcase your work.

Collaborative Development:

- **Real-time Collaboration:** Both platforms allow for real-time collaboration, meaning that multiple people can work on the same codebase simultaneously.

- **Version Control:** Even though online platforms like CodeSandbox and StackBlitz are great for quick development, you should consider integrating with version control tools like **GitHub** for larger projects, ensuring better code tracking and team collaboration.

Best Practices for Collaboration:

- **Clear Documentation:** Include a README file explaining the project and instructions for running the code, so your collaborators know how to interact with the project.

- **Issue Tracking:** Use GitHub issues or the built-in issue tracking system of CodeSandbox/StackBlitz to manage tasks and bugs efficiently.

- **Regular Updates:** Keep your project up-to-date and share progress with collaborators regularly to maintain alignment on goals.

13.2 Interactive Exercises

Hands-on learning is one of the most effective methods for mastering LangGraph.js. In this section, we will walk through **interactive exercises** that provide real-world challenges to help you solidify your understanding of agent workflows.

13.2.1 Hands-On Challenges

These challenges will test your understanding of LangGraph.js concepts by providing scenarios that require you to create and modify workflows.

Challenge 1: Building a Basic Workflow

- **Objective:** Create a simple LangGraph.js workflow with two agents: one that adds 5 to a number, and another that multiplies the result by 2.

Steps:

1. Create a workflow with two agents: one that adds 5 to a number and another that multiplies the result by 2.
2. Pass the number through both agents and log the final result.

Solution:

javascript

```javascript
graph.addAgent('AddFiveAgent', async (context) => {
  const number = context.data.number;
  context.data.result = number + 5;
  context.next();
});

graph.addAgent('MultiplyByTwoAgent', async (context) => {
  const result = context.data.result;
  context.data.finalResult = result * 2;
  context.next();
});

graph.run('simpleWorkflow', { number: 10 });
```

Explanation:

- The AddFiveAgent adds 5 to the number, and the MultiplyByTwoAgent multiplies the result by 2.
- The final result is 30, as (10 + 5) * 2 = 30.

Challenge 2: Creating a Simple Chatbot

- **Objective:** Build a chatbot that responds to simple greetings such as "Hello" and "How are you?"

Steps:

1. Define an agent that checks the user's message for greetings.
2. Respond with a predefined message based on the user's input.

Solution:

javascript

```javascript
graph.addAgent('GreetingAgent', async (context) => {
  const message = context.data.message;
  if (message.toLowerCase().includes('hello')) {
    context.data.response = 'Hello! How can I assist you today?';
  } else if (message.toLowerCase().includes('how are you')) {
    context.data.response = 'I'm doing great, thank you for asking!';
  } else {
    context.data.response = 'I didn't understand that.';
  }
  context.next();
});

graph.run('chatbotWorkflow', { message: 'Hello' });
```

Explanation:

- The GreetingAgent checks if the message includes specific keywords ("hello" or "how are you") and returns a response accordingly.

13.2.2 Real-Time Feedback and Solutions

Real-time feedback allows you to instantly see the results of your code and understand the impact of your changes. This feedback loop is essential for improving your skills and gaining confidence in your ability to design workflows.

Key Concepts:

- **Immediate Testing:** Platforms like CodeSandbox and StackBlitz provide live previews that update as you make changes to your code.
- **Error Detection:** These environments also display errors in real time, helping you quickly identify and fix problems.

Example: Real-Time Debugging

When you encounter issues in your workflow, the real-time environment will highlight syntax errors or undefined variables. For instance:

javascript

```javascript
graph.addAgent('GreetingAgent', async (context) => {
  context.data.messag = 'Hello'; // Typo here: "messag" should be "message"
  context.next();
});
```

Error Output:

- The IDE will flag the typo, making it clear that "messag" is not a defined property of context.data.

Best Practices for Real-Time Feedback:

- **Debugging Tools:** Use the debugging tools provided by the online IDEs to inspect variables and step through your code.

- **Iterative Testing:** Make small changes and test frequently to isolate issues and understand the effects of your changes.
- **Check Error Logs:** Always review the console for warnings and errors to ensure smooth execution.

13.3 Gamified Challenges for Workflow Design

Gamification turns learning into a fun and motivating experience. In this section, we explore how gamified challenges can be used to enhance your understanding of LangGraph.js and keep you engaged as you design more complex workflows.

13.3.1 Engaging Activities to Reinforce Learning

Gamified activities encourage problem-solving, quick thinking, and friendly competition. These activities can include:

- **Time-Based Challenges:** Complete a task in a set amount of time, such as building a workflow to process data or design an agent-based system.
- **Complexity Escalation:** Start with simpler tasks and work your way up to more complex scenarios that require integrating multiple agents and workflows.
- **Leveling Up:** Earn badges or points for completing challenges. As you tackle more difficult tasks, you unlock higher levels or achievements.

13.3.2 Leaderboards and Achievement Systems

Leaderboards and achievement systems provide recognition and reward for your progress. These systems track your performance across challenges, motivating you to complete more tasks and improve your skills.

Example: Badge System

- **"Workflow Beginner"** – Complete your first workflow.
- **"Agent Expert"** – Create 10 unique agents.

- **"Master Debugger"** – Successfully debug and solve 5 errors in your workflows.

Best Practices for Gamified Learning:

- **Set Realistic Goals:** Aim for achievable challenges that progressively increase in difficulty.
- **Compete and Collaborate:** Share your progress with others and engage in friendly competition.
- **Track Achievements:** Keep track of your progress and reward yourself for milestones.

Summary

In **Chapter 13**, we explored interactive learning with LangGraph.js through platforms like CodeSandbox and StackBlitz, providing hands-on exercises to reinforce your skills. You learned how to set up interactive coding environments, solve real-world challenges, and receive instant feedback on your progress. Additionally, gamified challenges added a fun element to your learning journey, allowing you to track your achievements and compete with others.

Chapter 14: The Future of Agent Workflows

The future of agent workflows is brimming with potential, as new technologies continue to emerge, and the demand for more intelligent, autonomous systems grows. LangGraph.js, as a flexible and powerful framework for agent-based workflows, is at the forefront of this evolution. In this chapter, we will explore the **emerging trends** in agent workflows, such as **decentralized AI systems** and **agent-based modeling in simulations**, and provide an overview of the **LangGraph.js roadmap**, including **upcoming features** and how **community contributions** are shaping the future of the framework.

14.1 Emerging Trends

As technology advances, new trends are shaping how we design and implement agent workflows. These trends highlight the growing complexity and versatility of agent-based systems, as well as the role of LangGraph.js in adapting to these innovations.

14.1.1 Decentralized AI Systems

Decentralized AI systems refer to a paradigm where intelligence is distributed across multiple nodes, rather than being controlled by a central authority. This approach can increase resilience, improve privacy, and enable more scalable systems. In decentralized systems, agents operate independently, often communicating and coordinating without relying on a central server.

Key Concepts:

- **Autonomous Agents:** Each agent can make decisions based on local information and interact with other agents to achieve a shared goal.

- **Blockchain and Distributed Ledger Technology (DLT):** Decentralized AI systems often integrate blockchain to ensure secure and transparent communication between agents.

- **Edge Computing:** With the rise of the Internet of Things (IoT) and edge devices, decentralized AI systems are increasingly deployed on devices at the "edge" of the network, minimizing latency and reducing dependency on centralized cloud servers.

Example: Decentralized Workflow in LangGraph.js

Imagine a scenario where agents are deployed across multiple devices in a smart city environment. Each agent makes autonomous decisions based on local data (e.g., traffic data, environmental conditions). These agents then communicate with each other to coordinate actions such as traffic light control, garbage collection, or energy consumption.

1. **Agent Definitions:**

javascript

```javascript
graph.addAgent('TrafficLightAgent', async (context) => {
  const trafficFlow = context.data.trafficFlow;  // Local data collected from traffic sensors
  if (trafficFlow > 80) {
    context.data.action = 'Red';  // Change light to red if traffic flow is high
  } else {
    context.data.action = 'Green';
  }
  context.next();
});

graph.addAgent('CityCoordinatorAgent', async (context) => {
  // The CityCoordinatorAgent collects actions from local agents and coordinates them
  const action = context.data.action;
  console.log(`City-wide action: ${action}`);
```

```
  context.next();
});

graph.defineWorkflow('smartCityWorkflow',
['TrafficLightAgent', 'CityCoordinatorAgent']);
```

Explanation:

- **TrafficLightAgent:** The agent operates autonomously, making decisions about the traffic light based on local traffic data.
- **CityCoordinatorAgent:** This agent aggregates actions from all traffic light agents in the city to ensure coordination.

Best Practices for Decentralized AI Systems:

- **Data Privacy:** Ensure that agents process data locally without transferring sensitive information to central servers.
- **Fault Tolerance:** Design systems where agents can continue operating even if some nodes go down, ensuring reliability.
- **Inter-Agent Communication:** Use protocols that allow efficient, secure communication between agents, such as message queues or peer-to-peer networks.

14.1.2 Agent-Based Modeling in Simulations

Agent-based modeling (ABM) is a powerful tool for simulating complex systems where individual agents interact within an environment. These models are used in fields ranging from economics and sociology to ecology and traffic management. LangGraph.js can be used to build agent-based simulations, where each agent is responsible for performing a task and interacting with other agents to simulate real-world systems.

Key Concepts:

- **Individual Behaviors:** Each agent in an ABM has specific rules and behaviors, allowing for detailed simulation of real-world processes.

- **Emergent Phenomena:** ABM can be used to model emergent phenomena, where the collective behavior of agents gives rise to complex patterns that are not explicitly programmed.

- **Simulation Environments:** ABM systems often simulate environments with interacting agents, allowing researchers and developers to study system dynamics and make predictions.

Example: Traffic Simulation Using LangGraph.js

In a traffic simulation, each car could be modeled as an agent, with rules that govern its movement, such as speed, braking, and decision-making at intersections. The agents (cars) interact with each other and the environment (roads and traffic lights) to simulate real-world traffic flow.

1. **Defining the Agents:**

javascript

```javascript
graph.addAgent('CarAgent', async (context) => {
  const car = context.data.car;
  if (car.needsToStop) {
    car.speed = 0;  // Stop the car if it needs to
    console.log(`Car ${car.id} is stopping.`);
  } else {
    car.speed = 60;  // Continue moving at 60 km/h
    console.log(`Car ${car.id} is moving at ${car.speed} km/h.`);
  }
  context.next();
});
```

```
graph.addAgent('TrafficLightAgent', async (context) => {
  const lightStatus = context.data.lightStatus;
  if (lightStatus === 'Red') {
    context.data.action = 'Stop all cars';
  } else {
    context.data.action = 'Allow cars to pass';
  }
  context.next();
});

graph.defineWorkflow('trafficSimulationWorkflow',
['CarAgent', 'TrafficLightAgent']);
```

Explanation:

- **CarAgent:** The CarAgent controls the movement of individual cars, checking whether they need to stop or continue moving.

- **TrafficLightAgent:** The TrafficLightAgent dictates whether cars are allowed to pass based on the status of traffic lights.

Best Practices for Agent-Based Modeling:

- **Simplified Agent Rules:** Start with simple rules for agent behaviors, and iteratively add complexity.

- **Environment Representation:** Accurately model the environment in which the agents operate, including all relevant factors like road conditions or weather.

- **Experimentation:** Use ABMs to experiment with different scenarios and study how changes in agent behavior or environmental conditions affect the system.

14.2 LangGraph.js Roadmap

LangGraph.js is constantly evolving, with new features being added and improvements being made by both the core team and the open-source community. In this section, we will look at the **upcoming**

features of LangGraph.js and explore how **community contributions** are driving the future development of the framework.

14.2.1 Upcoming Features

The LangGraph.js team is always working on new features that enhance the functionality of the framework. Some of the upcoming features include:

1. Improved Performance and Optimization:

- **Parallel Execution:** LangGraph.js is exploring ways to allow agents to run in parallel across multiple threads or processes to improve performance in large workflows.
- **Memory Management Enhancements:** As workflows grow in size, memory consumption can become a bottleneck. Future versions of LangGraph.js will include optimizations to better manage memory usage, especially in environments with large numbers of agents.

2. Expanded Integration Capabilities:

- **Integration with More AI Libraries:** LangGraph.js will support deeper integration with machine learning and AI frameworks, such as **TensorFlow.js**, **PyTorch.js**, and **scikit-learn**, enabling agents to utilize advanced models and perform more complex tasks.
- **IoT Support:** With the rise of IoT applications, LangGraph.js is looking to expand its capabilities for managing and processing data from IoT devices in real-time.

3. Enhanced Visualization Tools:

- **Graphical Workflow Visualizer:** A built-in tool to visualize agent workflows, helping users design and debug complex systems more easily.
- **Real-Time Dashboards:** Dashboards to display the performance and status of running workflows, useful for monitoring systems in production environments.

4. Decentralized Workflow Support:

- As decentralized systems become more common, LangGraph.js will introduce features that allow agents to work in a decentralized manner, such as peer-to-peer communication, distributed data storage, and blockchain integration.

14.2.2 Community Contributions

LangGraph.js is an open-source project, and its growth is largely driven by contributions from the community. Here's how you can get involved:

1. Reporting Issues and Suggesting Features:

- If you encounter a bug or have an idea for a new feature, you can submit issues or feature requests via the GitHub repository. This is a great way to help improve the framework.

2. Writing Documentation:

- High-quality documentation is crucial for helping users get started with LangGraph.js. If you have experience with the framework, consider contributing to the documentation to make it more comprehensive and accessible.

3. Developing Plugins and Integrations:

- LangGraph.js is highly extensible, and the community is encouraged to develop plugins and integrations with other libraries or frameworks. You can submit your plugins to the official repository or share them with the community.

4. Code Contributions:

- If you're a developer, you can fork the LangGraph.js repository and contribute new features, bug fixes, or performance improvements. By submitting pull requests, you can directly influence the evolution of LangGraph.js.

5. Community Engagement:

- Join the LangGraph.js community on forums, discussion boards, or chat platforms. Participate in conversations, share your use cases, and help others learn about the framework.

Summary

In **Chapter 14**, we explored the future of agent workflows, focusing on the **emerging trends** in the field, including decentralized AI systems and agent-based modeling in simulations. We also looked at the **LangGraph.js roadmap**, highlighting upcoming features such as improved performance, expanded integrations, and decentralized workflow support. Finally, we discussed the importance of **community contributions** and how you can get involved in shaping the future of LangGraph.js.

Key Takeaways:

- **Emerging Trends:** Decentralized AI systems and agent-based modeling are shaping the future of agent workflows.

- **LangGraph.js Roadmap:** Upcoming features will enhance performance, support machine learning, and introduce more visualization tools.

- **Community Contributions:** LangGraph.js relies on community involvement for its growth. You can contribute by reporting issues, writing documentation, developing plugins, and submitting code improvements.

Appendices

This section of the book includes supplementary material designed to help you deepen your understanding of LangGraph.js, troubleshoot issues, and expand your knowledge. Whether you're referencing the LangGraph.js API, looking for further resources, or seeking a quick guide to key terms and concepts, these appendices provide valuable tools and references to support your learning journey.

Appendix A: LangGraph.js API Reference

This appendix provides the **complete documentation** of key functions and methods available in LangGraph.js. The goal is to give developers a detailed understanding of the framework's core functionality, helping you leverage its capabilities effectively. Here, you'll find descriptions of functions for defining agents, creating workflows, managing data, and more.

Core LangGraph.js Functions

1. **Graph Class**

The Graph class is the heart of LangGraph.js, providing methods to define and run agent workflows.

- **new Graph()**
  Creates a new instance of the Graph class.

javascript

```
const graph = new Graph();
```

2. **graph.addAgent(name, agentFunction)**

Registers a new agent with a workflow. The agent function is a callback that is executed when the agent is triggered.

- **Parameters:**
  - name (String): The name of the agent.

- agentFunction (Function): The function that defines the agent's behavior.

javascript

```javascript
graph.addAgent('GreetingAgent', async (context) => {
  context.data.response = 'Hello!';
  context.next();
});
```

3. **graph.run(workflowName, initialData)**

Runs a defined workflow. This method triggers the agents in the workflow, passing data between them as defined by the workflow.

- **Parameters:**
  - workflowName (String): The name of the workflow to run.
  - initialData (Object): The initial data to pass to the workflow.

javascript

```javascript
graph.run('greetingWorkflow', { message: 'Hi there!' });
```

4. **graph.defineWorkflow(workflowName, agentNames)**

Defines a workflow by specifying the sequence of agents to run. Agents are executed in the order they are added.

- **Parameters:**
  - workflowName (String): The name of the workflow.
  - agentNames (Array): An array of agent names to be executed in sequence.

javascript

```javascript
graph.defineWorkflow('greetingWorkflow', ['GreetingAgent', 'FarewellAgent']);
```

Utility Functions

1. **context.next()**

This method is called by agents to signal that they have completed their task and the next agent can be executed.

```javascript
context.next();
```

2. **context.data**

This is the data object that agents can use to store and retrieve information during the execution of the workflow.

```javascript
context.data.message = 'Hello from LangGraph.js';
```

3. **graph.getAgent(name)**

Retrieves a registered agent by name, allowing you to inspect or modify its behavior.

```javascript
const agent = graph.getAgent('GreetingAgent');
```

Appendix B: Troubleshooting Guide

In this appendix, we will cover some of the most common issues you may encounter while working with LangGraph.js and provide solutions to help resolve them.

Common Issues and Their Fixes

1. **Issue: "Agent not executing as expected"**
    - **Solution:** Check the sequence of your agents in the workflow. Agents are executed in the order they are defined. Ensure that each agent calls context.next() to proceed to the next agent. If an agent doesn't call context.next(), the workflow will stop.

javascript

```javascript
graph.addAgent('MyAgent', async (context) => {
  // Perform actions
  context.next();  // Ensure this is called
});
```

2. **Issue: "Data not passing between agents"**
    - **Solution:** Ensure that you are correctly assigning data to context.data. Agents can only access and modify the data passed to them through the context object.

javascript

```javascript
graph.addAgent('AgentOne', async (context) => {
  context.data.number = 42;  // Set data
  context.next();
});

graph.addAgent('AgentTwo', async (context) => {
  console.log(context.data.number);  // Access data
});
```

3. **Issue: "Workflow not starting"**
    - **Solution:** Double-check the workflow definition and make sure the workflow is defined before attempting to run it. Ensure that you are calling graph.run() with the correct workflow name.

javascript

```javascript
graph.defineWorkflow('myWorkflow', ['AgentOne', 'AgentTwo']);
graph.run('myWorkflow', { initialData: true });
```

4. **Issue: "Unexpected behavior when using async functions"**
    - **Solution:** LangGraph.js supports asynchronous agent functions. Ensure that you are handling promises correctly, and using async/await when necessary.

javascript

```javascript
graph.addAgent('AsyncAgent', async (context) => {
  const result = await fetchData();  // Wait for the data
  context.data.result = result;
  context.next();
});
```

Appendix C: Resources and Further Reading

To continue your learning journey with LangGraph.js, here are some recommended resources that can provide further insight into agent-based systems, JavaScript frameworks, and best practices for building workflows.

Recommended Books:

- **"Designing Multi-Agent Systems"** by Michael Wooldridge
  A comprehensive guide to designing and building multi-agent systems, with foundational concepts relevant to LangGraph.js.

- **"JavaScript: The Good Parts"** by Douglas Crockford
  This book offers a deep dive into JavaScript's most powerful and elegant features, which will help you write more efficient LangGraph.js code.

Blogs and Articles:

- **LangGraph.js Blog (Official)**
  The official LangGraph.js blog provides updates, tutorials, and case studies that can help you stay up to date with the latest features and techniques.

- **Medium Articles on Agent-Based Modeling**
  Explore various articles on Medium that delve into the theory and practical applications of agent-based modeling, which can be applied to LangGraph.js workflows.

Research Papers:

- **"Agent-Based Models and Simulations"** by Michael A. Bodenhamer
  A paper that explores the use of agent-based models in simulations and how this approach can be leveraged to model real-world systems.

- **"Multi-Agent Systems for Distributed Problem Solving"** by Roger M. Lee
  A scholarly paper on how multi-agent systems are used in distributed problem-solving, providing background that can inform more complex LangGraph.js workflows.

Appendix D: Cheat Sheets

This section provides quick reference guides to help you quickly recall LangGraph.js concepts and commands while developing your workflows. This cheat sheet will cover the most common and useful commands.

LangGraph.js Cheat Sheet

1. **Creating a Graph:**

javascript

```
const graph = new Graph();
```

2. **Defining an Agent:**

javascript

```javascript
graph.addAgent('AgentName', async (context) => {
  // Agent logic
  context.next();
});
```

3. **Running a Workflow:**

javascript

```javascript
graph.run('workflowName', { initialData: true });
```

4. **Defining a Workflow:**

javascript

```javascript
graph.defineWorkflow('workflowName', ['AgentOne', 'AgentTwo']);
```

5. **Accessing Data in Agents:**

javascript

```javascript
const data = context.data;
context.data.result = 42;  // Modify data
```

6. **Handling Asynchronous Agents:**

javascript

```javascript
graph.addAgent('AsyncAgent', async (context) => {
  const data = await fetchData();
  context.data.result = data;
  context.next();
});
```

Appendix E: Glossary of Terms

This glossary provides definitions of key terms and concepts that are important for working with LangGraph.js.

Key Terms:

1. **Agent:**
   An independent unit within a workflow that performs specific tasks based on the rules defined within it.

2. **Workflow:**
   A sequence of agents defined to execute in a specific order to accomplish a task or process.

3. **Context:**
   An object that stores and shares data between agents within a workflow. Agents use the context to read and modify data.

4. **Graph:**
   The central structure in LangGraph.js, responsible for defining, running, and managing workflows and agents.

5. **Asynchronous Agent:**
   An agent that performs tasks asynchronously, using promises or async/await syntax.

6. **Decentralized Systems:**
   Systems where decision-making and processing are distributed across multiple independent nodes, rather than relying on a central controller.

7. **Agent-Based Modeling (ABM):**
   A method for simulating complex systems where individual agents interact based on specific rules to create emergent behaviors.

Conclusion

Congratulations! By making it this far, you've embarked on an exciting journey to master **LangGraph.js**, the framework at the cutting edge of agent-based workflows and multi-agent systems. Whether you're a web developer, an AI enthusiast, or someone looking to build real-time, intelligent systems, this book has equipped you with the tools, techniques, and insights needed to create sophisticated workflows with LangGraph.js.

Throughout this book, you've learned not just how to use LangGraph.js, but how to extend it, integrate it with other powerful libraries, and apply it to real-world problems. From building simple workflows to creating complex multi-agent systems, from working with AI integrations to scaling applications, every chapter has provided you with hands-on projects and real-world scenarios to enhance your skills.

But more importantly, **LangGraph.js is not just about writing code—it's about shaping the future**. The world of agent-based workflows is growing rapidly, and by mastering LangGraph.js, you're not just keeping up with current trends; you're paving the way for the next generation of decentralized AI systems, real-time data processing, and complex simulations. You are part of a larger movement that is making systems smarter, more autonomous, and capable of solving problems we haven't even thought of yet.

As you reflect on what you've learned, remember that **LangGraph.js is only as powerful as the creativity you bring to it**. The ideas and workflows you design today could be the foundation of groundbreaking systems tomorrow. So, we encourage you to keep experimenting, building, and innovating. The world of agent-based systems is vast, and LangGraph.js is a framework that can scale with you as your ideas evolve.

I hope you feel confident not only in your ability to create workflows but in your ability to contribute to the community. The future of LangGraph.js depends on passionate developers like you who will build upon it, extend it, and share it with others. Whether you're reporting a bug, submitting a new plugin, or just discussing ideas with fellow developers, you're helping shape the trajectory of this powerful tool.

I'd love for you to share your journey! **Leave a review**—tell me what you loved about the book, which sections helped you the most, and what you'd like to see in future editions. Share your projects, your ideas, and your experiences with others who are just as excited as you are to explore LangGraph.js.

And most importantly, **talk about this book**. Share it with your friends, colleagues, and fellow developers who are ready to dive into the world of agent-based workflows and multi-agent systems. Spread the word about how LangGraph.js is empowering developers and shaping the future of intelligent systems.

Your journey doesn't end here. It's only just beginning.

I wish you success in all your future LangGraph.js projects and beyond. Keep creating, keep experimenting, and keep pushing the boundaries of what's possible!

I'd love to hear from you. Follow me on amazon to get notified anytime I drop any body of work, share your feedback, and let's continue the conversation!

www.ingramcontent.com/pod-product-compliance
Lightning Source LLC
Chambersburg PA
CBHW062101220526
45471CB00010B/3562